An Analysis of

Thomas
Robert Malthus's

An Essay on the
Principle of Population

Nick Broten

Published by Macat International Ltd
24:13 Coda Centre, 189 Munster Road, London SW6 6AW.

Distributed exclusively by Routledge
2 Park Square, Milton Park, Abingdon, Oxon OX14 4RN
711 Third Avenue, New York, NY 10017, USA

Routledge is an imprint of the Taylor & Francis Group, an informa business

www.macat.com
info@macat.com

Cataloguing in Publication Data
A catalogue record for this book is available from the British Library.
Library of Congress Cataloguing-in-Publication Data is available upon request.
Cover illustration: Etienne Gilfillan

ISBN 978-1-912302-29-1 (hardback)
ISBN 978-1-912127-78-8 (paperback)
ISBN 978-1-912281-17-6 (e-book)

CONTENTS

THE MACAT LIBRARY

The Macat Library is a series of unique academic explorations of seminal works in the humanities and social sciences – books and papers that have had a significant and widely recognised impact on their disciplines. It has been created to serve as much more than just a summary of what lies between the covers of a great book. It illuminates and explores the influences on, ideas of, and impact of that book. Our goal is to offer a learning resource that encourages critical thinking and fosters a better, deeper understanding of important ideas.

Each publication is divided into three Sections: Influences, Ideas, and Impact. Each Section has four Modules. These explore every important facet of the work, and the responses to it.

This Section-Module structure makes a Macat Library book easy to use, but it has another important feature. Because each Macat book is written to the same format, it is possible (and encouraged!) to cross-reference multiple Macat books along the same lines of inquiry or research. This allows the reader to open up interesting interdisciplinary pathways.

To further aid your reading, lists of glossary terms and people mentioned are included at the end of this book (these are indicated by an asterisk [*] throughout) – as well as a list of works cited.

Macat has worked with the University of Cambridge to identify the elements of critical thinking and understand the ways in which six different skills combine to enable effective thinking.
Three allow us to fully understand a problem; three more give us the tools to solve it. Together, these six skills make up the **PACIER** model of critical thinking. They are:

ANALYSIS – understanding how an argument is built
EVALUATION – exploring the strengths and weaknesses of an argument
INTERPRETATION – understanding issues of meaning

CREATIVE THINKING – coming up with new ideas and fresh connections
PROBLEM-SOLVING – producing strong solutions
REASONING – creating strong arguments

To find out more, visit **WWW.MACAT.COM.**

CRITICAL THINKING AND
AN ESSAY ON THE PRINCIPLE OF POPULATION

Primary critical thinking skill: REASONING
Secondary critical thinking skill: PROBLEM-SOLVING

Thomas Robert Malthus' 1798 *Essay on the Principle of Population* helped change the direction of economics, politics, and the natural sciences with its reasoning and problem solving.

The central topic of the essay was the idea, extremely prevalent in the 18th and 19th centuries, that human society was in some way perfectible. According to many thinkers of the time, mankind was on a course of steady improvement with advances set to continuously improve society and life for all. Malthus was a skeptic on this point, and, in a clear example of the skill of reasoning, set about constructing and marshalling a strong argument for a less optimistic view.

Central to his argument were the laws of population growth and their relationship to growth in agricultural production; in his view the former would always outstrip the latter. This provided a strong argument that society was limited by finite resources – a closely reasoned argument that continues to influence economists, politicians and scientists today, as well as environmental movements. While Malthus' proposed solutions have been less influential, they remain an excellent example of problem solving, offering a range of answers to the problem of population growth and finite resources.

ABOUT THE AUTHOR OF THE ORIGINAL WORK

Thomas Robert Malthus was born in 1766 in Dorking, England—a country town just south of London. After studying at Cambridge, he began his working life as an assistant to a clergyman. Malthus published his most important work, An Essay on the Principle of Population, in 1798, arguing that population growth will always outstrip the availability of food if unchecked. Malthus was a renowned political economist in his day and from 1805 worked as professor of history and political economy at East India Company College, near London. He died in 1834 at the age of 68.

ABOUT THE AUTHOR OF THE ANALYSIS

Nick Broten was educated at the London School of Economics and the California Institute of Technology. He is doing postgraduate work at the Pardee RAND Graduate School and works as an assistant policy analyst at RAND. His current policy interests include designing distribution methods for end-of-life care, closing labour market skill gaps, and understanding biases in risk-taking by venture capitalists.

ABOUT MACAT

GREAT WORKS FOR CRITICAL THINKING

Macat is focused on making the ideas of the world's great thinkers accessible and comprehensible to everybody, everywhere, in ways that promote the development of enhanced critical thinking skills.

It works with leading academics from the world's top universities to produce new analyses that focus on the ideas and the impact of the most influential works ever written across a wide variety of academic disciplines. Each of the works that sit at the heart of its growing library is an enduring example of great thinking. But by setting them in context – and looking at the influences that shaped their authors, as well as the responses they provoked – Macat encourages readers to look at these classics and game-changers with fresh eyes. Readers learn to think, engage and challenge their ideas, rather than simply accepting them.

WAYS IN TO THE TEXT

KEY POINTS

- The English political economist Thomas Robert Malthus (1766–1834) was one of the most influential thinkers of his time. His work has been cited by many important figures including Charles Darwin* and John Maynard Keynes.*

- The central claim of the *Essay* is that human progress will always be constrained by curbs to population growth.

- The book is an early example, one of the first of many, of how scientific principles can be applied to social problems. Its influence can still be felt today.

Who Was Thomas Robert Malthus?

Thomas Robert Malthus was a British political economist, philosopher, and demographer.* He is best known for developing the principle that population growth and social progress are naturally in conflict. *An Essay on the Principle of Population*, in which Malthus examines this idea, has been widely influential and still impacts today's political and economic discourse.[1]

Malthus was born in 1766 in Dorking, England—a country town just south of London. After secondary education at a dissenting academy,* a school for members of a minority Protestant sect, Malthus studied mathematics at Cambridge University. He graduated in 1788 and accepted a position as curate—a member of the clergy who assists priests—at Oakwood Chapel in the parish of Wotton, Surrey.

At the age of 32, Malthus published the first edition of the *Essay*. The *Essay* was a response to a pamphlet published by radical British philosopher William Godwin,* entitled *An Enquiry Concerning Political Justice*.[2] In it, Godwin suggested that eliminating existing political institutions—as revolutionaries were attempting to do in France at the time—would ultimately liberate and enlighten society. The population principle Malthus developed in the *Essay* was meant to refute this idea, by claiming that calamities due to overpopulation are inevitable. This suggests the need for strong institutions to keep order. Malthus and Godwin maintained an intellectual dialogue throughout their careers.

Between the publication of the first edition of the *Essay* in 1798 and his death in 1834, Malthus refined his ideas as more evidence and a wider discussion of the subject became available. Throughout his career, Malthus accompanied his work on population with wider studies into political economy (which we now call economics), and from 1805 he maintained a position as Professor of History and Political Economy at East India Company College, near London.

The strength of Malthus's argument in the *Essay* gave him a wide and influential audience. Charles Darwin, the famous British naturalist, cited the *Essay* as a key inspiration for his theory of evolution.[3] In addition, the twentieth-century British economist John Maynard Keynes widely praised Malthus's approach to political economy. Malthus even inspired innovations in how mathematicians model life expectancy. However, his reception was not all positive. Karl Marx,* the German philosopher and one of the most influential political thinkers of the nineteenth century, was an outspoken critic, calling the work "school-boyish."[4] Nevertheless, the *Essay* remains influential. Today, a new breed of writers—loosely known as "neo-Malthusians"— have reinterpreted his basic premise as a warning about the environmental and social impacts of overpopulation.

What Does *An Essay on the Principle of Population* Say?

The main idea in Malthus's *Essay* is that, over time, population growth will always outstrip the availability of food. He argued that, unchecked, population will grow according to the sequence 1, 2, 4, 8, 16—that is, exponentially. In contrast, agricultural production will at best grow following the sequence 1, 2, 3, 4, 5—in a linear fashion, or until all resources are used up.[5] Eventually, demand for food will outstrip what the land can produce, thereby causing the population to decline from disease and famine.

Malthus made this shocking claim at a time when most thinkers felt economic growth and human progress went hand in hand with increases in population. Malthus proposed a new way of thinking about the issue. He used a scientific approach to examine the ways in which curbs on population—sickness and death caused by food shortages—influence human welfare. Even Malthus himself appeared to be somewhat uneasy with this idea and softened his views somewhat in later editions of the book. Yet his *Essay* was used as an argument against the Poor Laws,* social welfare programs that were in place in England between the sixteenth and twentieth centuries, to provide some relief to the very poor. Malthus suggested that such help was pointless since it only encouraged population growth and would therefore lead to further misery.

Most economists agree that Malthus's model provided an accurate description of the world before about 1800. But they generally feel it no longer applies to today's developed countries where technological advances have increased food production in ways that Malthus did not foresee. Yet his concerns about the problems related to overpopulation continue to shape public debate. Some current supporters of Malthus's views believe that the kind of dramatic famine hinted at in his *Essay* remains a threat to global society. American biologists Paul and Anne Ehrlich,* two outspoken followers of Malthus, have suggested that we are using up the earth's resources at a dangerous rate. "Careful analysis … does not provide much confidence that technology will save us or that gross domestic product can be disengaged from resource use."[6] They warn that more must be done to avoid catastrophe: put more land into agricultural use, improve soil conservation, develop better fertilizers and agricultural techniques, and reduce food waste. Otherwise, the planet will be unable to produce enough food to meet the needs of the population. While not mainstream, this view represents of some of the current concerns about population that echo Malthus's ideas.

Malthus's *Essay* is also important for understanding the potential implications for human society of climate change. The *availability* of food—central to Malthus's ideas—is closely linked to climate. For example, research has shown that global warming may reduce crop yields. This has worrying implications for future food security—our ability to reliably produce enough food for the population.[7] There are other examples of the strained relationship between human practices and food production. Take the current concern about the extinction of some bee populations, which many scientists think may have been caused by man-made pesticides. Pollination of plants by bees is responsible for billions of dollars of crop yields in the United States alone. If what is known as "colony collapse disorder"* continues, agricultural yields may drop further.[8]

Some of Malthus's ideas have been proven to be wrong—in the nearly two centuries since his death, food production has kept up with rapid population growth in most parts of the world. Yet his idea about how population grows and its relationship to food supplies is fundamental to the way society functions. Reading and understanding the *Essay* is an important step towards being able to interpret population and income issues, both now and in the future.

Why Does *An Essay on the Principle of Population* Matter?

Malthus's *Essay* is an exercise in applying scientific principles to social problems.

He used careful observations to construct well-argued theories about how society works. Ideally, the reader gains an appreciation of this kind of modeling—the cornerstone of modern social science—by working through Malthus's relatively simple population model.

Malthus's *Essay* is a good starting point for thinking about social science modeling for at least two reasons. First, it is an early example of such a model, and many later developments took place after considering Malthus's population principle. For example, the widely known economic concept of diminishing marginal utility* is considered to have emerged almost directly from Malthus's population model as follows. Malthus reasoned that as population increases, more land must be cultivated for food. But since the best agricultural land is always used first, each additional piece of land is likely to be less productive. As demand continues growing, farmers turn to ever-poorer soils and the yield for each new acre—i.e., the marginal utility of the land—keeps diminishing.

Second, Malthus's population principle can be stated and understood using only the most basic mathematics. In contrast, many ideas in modern economics and demography—the statistical study of human population—require complex mathematical equations in order to be fully understood. It is a testament to the strength of Malthus's argument that he was able to produce such a strong conclusion from basic concepts.

Learning to construct well-reasoned arguments from basic principles will benefit all readers of the *Essay*—not only those with an interest in social science. Perhaps the greatest proof of this is Charles Darwin's testimonial after reading the work: "I happened to read for amusement Malthus on *Population*, and being well prepared to appreciate the struggle for existence which everywhere goes on from long-continued observation of the habits of animals and plants, it at once struck me that under these circumstances favorable variations would tend to be preserved, and unfavorable ones destroyed … Here, then, I had at last got a theory by which to work."[9] Just as Darwin found an application of Malthus's logic in evolutionary biology, readers will find areas in all aspects of life to which they can apply the logic of Malthus's argument.

NOTES

1   Donald Winch, *Malthus: A Very Short Introduction* (Oxford: Oxford University Press, 2013).

2   Thomas Robert Malthus, *An Essay on the Principle of Population*, ed. Donald Winch (Cambridge: Cambridge University Press, 1992), 56.

3   Nora Barlow, ed., *The Autobiography of Charles Darwin: 1809–1882* (New York: Norton, 1958), 120.

4   Karl Marx, "Capital – Footnote to Part VII, Chapter 25, Section I," in *An Essay on the Principle of Population: Text, Sources and Background, Criticism*, ed. Philip Appleman (New York: Norton, 1976), 159.

5   Malthus, *Essay*, 19.

6   Paul R. Ehrlich and Anne H. Ehrlich, "Can a Collapse of Global Civilization Be Avoided?" *Proceedings of the Royal Society: Biological Sciences* 280, no. 1754 (2013), accessed February 2, 2015, doi:10.1098/rspb.2012.2845.

7   Martin Parry, "The Implications of Climate Change for Crop Yields, Global Food Supply and Risk of Hunger," *International Crops Research Institute for the Semi-Arid Tropics eJournal* (2007), accessed October 1, 2013, www.icrisat.org/journal/SpecialProject/sp14.pdf.

8   Bryan Walsh, "The Trouble with Beekeeping in the Anthropocene," *Time*, August 9, 2013, accessed October 1, 2013, http://science.time.com/2013/08/09/the-trouble-with-beekeeping-in-the-anthropocene/.

9   Barlow, *Autobiography*, 120.

SECTION 1
INFLUENCES

MODULE 1
THE AUTHOR AND THE
HISTORICAL CONTEXT

KEY POINTS

- Malthus's *Essay* is relevant to current debates over whether expanding population—and human activities—could overstretch the earth's capacity to provide enough food and clean water.

- Malthus was trained in mathematics and exposed to Isaac Newton's* principle of scientific inquiry, and the French Revolution.*

- Malthus's father was friendly with Jean-Jacques Rousseau,* whose ideas on the perfectibility of society became a focus for Malthus.

Why Read This Text?

Thomas Robert Malthus's *An Essay on the Principle of Population*, published in 1798, has had a wide-ranging and lasting impact on the social sciences, from economics to demography,* and is one of the most influential publications in modern history. As economists Ran Abramitzky and Fabio Braggion noted in their review of Malthus's work, "Few economists have had such controversial ideas, and generated a debate on such a scale, as Thomas Malthus."[1] The centerpiece of this debate is Malthus's population model, which states that population growth and social and economic progress are naturally in conflict because an expanding population will inevitably be curbed by the limitations of our ability to produce enough food. Readers of the *Essay* will discover that, while Malthus's ideas have been challenged repeatedly in the nearly two centuries since his death, they remain an important part of public discussions.

❝ Robert Malthus's name is chiefly and irrevocably linked with what he was the first to present as a universal and perpetual dilemma: He maintained that the prospects for permanent improvement in the condition of the mass of society in all countries was placed in a precarious balance by an unequal race between the hare of population growth and a tortoise representing the power to expand food production. ❞

Donald Winch, *Malthus: A Very Short Introduction*

Author's Life

Relatively little is known about Malthus's life prior to the first edition of the *Essay*, but a few facts from the period shed light on his most famous work. His father, Daniel Malthus, was described as "eccentric" and "scattered," but he maintained a deep interest in wide-ranging intellectual pursuits, from botany to foreign literature.[2] Perhaps most important, Daniel was a friend and admirer of the Genevan philosopher Jean-Jacques Rousseau—one of Malthus's targets in the *Essay*.

One unusual feature of Malthus's life—and evidence of Daniel Malthus's eccentricity—was his father's decision to send him to a dissenting academy* at the age of 16. Students at dissenting academies were typically excluded from traditional English universities, so it is somewhat surprising that Malthus gained admission to Cambridge University, where he studied from 1784. While at Cambridge, Malthus studied mathematics—an influence that is apparent in the *Essay*, as he draws crucially on the concepts of geometric and arithmetic series.

Upon leaving Cambridge in 1788, Malthus was immediately ordained and took a post as curate—a member of the clergy—in the chapel of Oakwood in the parish of Wotton, Surrey, which was close enough to his birthplace of Dorking for him to live in his family home. In 1793, Malthus was elected to a non-residential fellowship at Jesus College, Cambridge, which allowed him the freedom to pursue intellectual ambitions. One product of this period was his pamphlet "The Crisis, a View of the Present State of Great Britain, by a Friend of the Constitution," which was Malthus's first attempt at a political essay. However, it was never published.

Author's Background

Although Malthus conceived the *Essay* in the comfort of his country home, he wrote it at a time of intellectual and political upheaval in England and Europe, and this context reveals itself in the text. Most important, Malthus was influenced by the Enlightenment* ideal of applying scientific principles to understand the workings of human society, in the same way that Isaac Newton, who is considered one of the most important scientists in history, applied scientific principles to understand the natural world. Malthus believed that understanding social problems required observation of the unchangeable laws of nature. He wrote in the *Essay* that the constancy of the laws of nature, and of effects and causes, are "the foundation for all human knowledge."[3]

Another important feature of the context in which Malthus worked was the French Revolution, which played a significant role in the political and intellectual debates of the late eighteenth century. While Malthus was insulated from the direct consequences of the Revolution, his ideas were shaped by the British intellectual response to it. Some Enlightenment radicals viewed the Revolution as evidence that liberated societies built on the principles of reason could achieve a form of Utopia*—a "perfect" society. In contrast, conservatives viewed the Revolution as a reflection of social decay.[4] It's important to note that, prior to Malthus's contribution, both sides of the debate were largely moralistic, rather than based on scientific principle or fact.

Malthus thoroughly endorsed the Enlightenment ideals related to Newton's scientific method*—namely that there are laws governing nature and society that can be understand by careful observation. But he never endorsed the Utopian radical movement that accompanied the Revolution in France. Nor did he fully endorse the conservatism of some of its critics. Instead, his intellectual life appears to have been a "quest for a middle way between opposed doctrines"—embracing reason and logic, while applying those tools to curb the enthusiasm of the most radical adherents of the period's passionately held ideas.[5]

NOTES

1   Ran Abramitzky and Fabio Braggion, "Malthusian and Neo-Malthusian Theories," in *The Oxford Encyclopedia of Economic History*, ed. Joel Mokyr (Oxford: Oxford University Press, 2003), 1.

2   Donald Winch, *Malthus: A Very Short Introduction* (Oxford: Oxford University Press, 2013), 11.

3   Thomas Robert Malthus, *An Essay on the Principle of Population*, ed. Donald Winch (Cambridge: Cambridge University Press, 1992), 51.

4   Winch, *Malthus,* 11.

5   Winch, *Malthus*, 18.

MODULE 2
ACADEMIC CONTEXT

KEY POINTS

- The primary goal of political economy, as defined by Malthus, is to uncover the natural laws that govern social interactions.

- When Malthus was writing, the study of moral philosophy with its abstract ideas was being replaced by the more scientific approach of political economy.

- Malthus had only limited involvement with the dominant political economy thinkers of the time when he first wrote about his population principle, but over the course of his career he became a prominent political economist.

The Work in Its Context

As a country curate, Thomas Robert Malthus was not directly linked to any academic discipline while he was writing *An Essay on the Principle of Population*, and his interests were broad. Throughout the text, he addresses questions that would today be covered by fields as diverse as mathematics, sociology, demography,* economics, and philosophy. Malthus would probably have considered his work a contribution to the field of political economy and moral philosophy. The text was published at a time when moral philosophy was giving way to the more systematic discipline of political economy.[1] Scholars were turning from basing their arguments on moral arguments to finding evidence in the real world to support their conclusions.

In general, political economists during Malthus's time were interested in uncovering the laws that governed society. This contrasted with the natural philosophers, who were concerned with the laws of the natural world. As the field of political economy was largely

> ❝ If everything else be equal, it seems natural to expect
> that wherever there are most happiness and virtue and
> the wisest institutions, there will also be most people. ❞
>
> David Hume,* "Of the Populousness of Ancient Nations"

undeveloped, the range of questions that scholars were asking was broad: What trade policies maximize national wealth? What causes inequality, and can total equality be achieved and sustained? What social policies will minimize the effects of inequality and maximize national welfare? How do agricultural practices, population, and wages interact? One important preoccupation of writers during this time—which Malthus addressed in the *Essay*—was the question of whether social outcomes are shaped by human nature or by laws and rules that a country adopts.[2]

The sub-topic of population to which most of the *Essay* is dedicated was of minor interest to the political economists and philosophers who preceded Malthus. They mostly approached the problem from an institutional perspective: Where institutions (the legal system, the civil service, schools, etc.) are strong, populations will flourish, and where institutions are weak, populations will decline. Writers tended to view population growth as a factor that accompanied favorable economic conditions, rather than as a threat to prosperity. These writers included David Hume in the mid-eighteenth century, and Adam Smith a quarter of a century later—both hugely influential Scottish philosophers and political economists. As Hume wrote: "If everything else be equal, it seems natural to expect that wherever there are most happiness and virtue and the wisest institutions, there will also be most people."[3]

Overview of the Field

The change from moral philosophy to political economy that occurred in the late eighteenth century was largely due to the work of

Adam Smith. His 1776 *An Enquiry into the Nature and Causes of the Wealth of Nations* was arguably the first text to systematically describe how economies work, and it is said to have created the "raw material for modern economics."[4] Before Smith's book was published, the dominant theory of political economy was mercantilism—a theory that generally stated that economies are most effective when serving the state.

Smith overturned this idea. He developed a theory that said the economy works best when it is guided by "self interest." When business-owners try to maximize their profits, and consumers are free to seek the best goods at the lowest prices, resources are used in the most efficient way. Decisions are left up to individuals and there is no central plan. Yet the economy is in balance, as if guided by an "invisible hand,"* as Smith famously stated.

Smith and Malthus were among the leading thinkers of a period in Europe known as the Enlightenment.* One of the central new ideas of the time was that both the natural world and society are governed by natural laws (and not by God's will)—which can be discovered through careful observation.[5] To the political economist, natural laws do not refer to value judgments, but to a set of unchanging rules that shape how the world works. So the purpose of scientific inquiry is to uncover these laws by applying the principles of Newton's scientific method.*

Academic Influences

At the time Malthus published the *Essay*, the major universities in England dominated intellectual debate—predominantly Oxford, Cambridge, and Edinburgh, all of which had close connections to the Church. Interestingly, Oxford and Cambridge did not recognize political economy as a field of study at the time, and when Malthus later took a professorship in political economy, it was at the significantly less reputable East India Company College.[6] It is unclear what kind of academic support Malthus had while composing the first edition of the *Essay* and what kinds of relationships he developed within the academic institutions to which he was attached. However, it is likely that his earlier position as Fellow at Jesus College, Cambridge, provided some access to influential academic networks.

Much of the intellectual debate outside of universities was carried out in pamphlets and newsletters, and the current distinctions between books versus pamphlets, and academic versus popular, were then undeveloped.[7] In fact, publishing houses would often publish, print, and sell the work from the same site. Because of this, the publishing industry at the time was highly informal, and one's ability to get into print was likely to be based on name recognition in the community and a previous record of popular publications.[8] Again, it is unknown how much influence Malthus had with publishers, although it should be noted that his first attempt at publication was declined. Added to that, when he eventually did publish the first edition of the *Essay* in 1798, he did so anonymously.[9]

NOTES

1   William Petersen, *Malthus: Founder of Modern Demography* (New Brunswick, N.J.: Transaction Publishers, 1999), 2.

2   Petersen, *Malthus*, 5.

3   David Hume, "Of the Populousness of Ancient Nations" (1752), in *An Essay on the Principle of Population: Text, Sources and Background, Criticism*, ed. Philip Appleman (New York: Norton, 1976), 3.

4   Petersen, *Malthus*, 8.

5   Petersen, *Malthus*, 5.

6   Petersen, *Malthus*, 29.

7   Petersen, *Malthus*, 16.

8   Petersen, *Malthus*, 16.

9   Petersen, *Malthus*, 29.

MODULE 3
THE PROBLEM

KEY POINTS

- The main question Malthus's *Essay* addresses is: can society be perfected?

- Philosophers Marquis de Condorcet and William Godwin* believed society can be perfected because the removal of inhibitive laws enables new social forms to emerge.

- Malthus rejected the view that society can be perfected, arguing that progress is inherently inhibited by selfish human tendencies.

Core Question

Thomas Robert Malthus wrote *An Essay on the Principle of Population* to provide an answer to the following question: is it possible for society to be perfected—i.e., to evolve into a form where misery, exploitation, and conflict are replaced by fulfillment and harmony? While this question appears to be philosophical, it had important political implications in the late eighteenth century. Specifically, a group of radical Utopian* thinkers in France and Britain viewed the French Revolution* as a step towards a more perfect society because they believed that irrational political institutions, like the monarchy, would give way to a rational social order.[1]

These radicals argued that political institutions of the kind being challenged by the Revolution in France were primarily responsible for restricting human advancement. They believed that removing those institutions and leaving people to govern themselves would give rise to a society with "no war, no crimes, no administration of justice, and no government ... [and] neither disease, anguish, melancholy, or resentment."[2]

> ❝ The aim of the work that I have undertaken, and its results, will be to show by appeal to reason and fact that nature has set no term to the perfection of human faculties; that the perfectibility of man is truly indefinite; and that the progress of this perfectibility, from now onwards independent of any power that might wish to halt it, has no other limits than the duration of the globe upon which nature has cast us. ❞
>
> Marquis de Condorcet,* "Sketch for a Historical Picture of the Progress of the Human Mind"

To conservatives—Malthus included—those suggestions were not only wrong, but also dangerous. Practically speaking, the political proposals of radical Utopians included removing institutions such as law, private property, and marriage. In contrast, Malthus believed those institutions were essential for progress in society. One example is Malthus's defense of private property: "It is to the established administration of property ... that we are indebted for all the noblest exertions of human genius ... for everything, indeed, that distinguishes the civilized from the savage state."[3]

Further, Malthus did not believe in the basic belief that human nature is essentially rational and therefore capable of perfection. Rather, as Donald Winch (a key biographer of Malthus) wrote, he believed that "our efforts to improve might grow stronger, but we shall not succeed in eliminating vice."[4] In that sense, Malthus viewed himself as a realist. While radicals believed that society could somehow transform human nature, Malthus believed society would always be under the influence of the most selfish human impulses.

The Participants

Jean-Jacques Rousseau* first proposed the idea of perfectibility of society in his *Discourse on Inequality*, published in 1754. However, it was not until the French Revolution (1789–1799), and the appearance of Rousseau's disciples, William Godwin and the French philosopher and mathematician Marquis de Condorcet, that the question became widely discussed. This was partly due to the adoption by Godwin and Condorcet of the view that society could be analyzed the same way that scientists study nature. This use of the scientific method seemed to challenge Malthus, who was also interested in applying scientific principles to social behavior.

For example, Condorcet wrote: "If man can … predict phenomena when he knows their laws, why, then, should it be regarded as a fantastic undertaking to sketch, with some pretense to truth, the future destiny of man on the basis of his history?"[5] Condorcet's interpretation of human history and its future potential was very positive. To him, a natural law of human society was the gradual movement towards greater prosperity, equality, and intellectual advancement. As American scholar William Petersen wrote: "If man is inherently as good as Condorcet and Godwin held, then no state is needed to maintain order; the anarchism* they professed" would be enough.[6]

The question of population growth is largely absent from the debate about perfectibility, except for one brief mention in Godwin's *Enquiry Concerning Political Justice* (1793). Godwin fleetingly observed: "There is a principle in human society by which population is perpetually kept down to the level of the means of subsistence."[7] This brief passage appears to be the seed from which Malthus's population principle grew.

The Contemporary Debate

Malthus's *Essay* is a direct response to Godwin's *Political Justice*, though he also reserves space for a response to Condorcet. While Malthus does not appear to have had a relationship with Condorcet, he and Godwin maintained a dialogue, both in public and private, throughout their lives. An interesting feature of the discussions between Malthus and

Godwin is that, while both began their intellectual lives at opposite extremes—Godwin a Utopian radical and Malthus strongly opposed to such radicalism—both moved towards the broadly accepted middle ground during their lifetimes.[8]

Another notable relationship of Malthus's early life was his father's friendship with Rousseau. Daniel Malthus was a strong supporter of Rousseau, and the earliest versions of the *Essay* appear to have been conceived as conversation pieces between Malthus and his father on the topic of human perfectibility—a subject on which they disagreed. While Rousseau was only loosely linked to those discussions, it is possible to imagine that if Daniel had not had a relationship with Rousseau, his son may never have developed his population theory.

NOTES

1   William Petersen, *Malthus: Founder of Modern Demography* (New Brunswick, N.J.: Transaction Publishers, 1979), 5.

2   William Godwin, *Enquiry Concerning Political Justice and Its Influence on Morals and Happiness* (London: G.G. and J. Robinson, 1798), 528.

3   Donald Winch, *Malthus: A Very Short Introduction* (Oxford: Oxford University Press, 2013), 58.

4   Winch, *Malthus*, 32.

5   Marquis de Condorcet, "Sketch for a Historical Picture of the Progress of the Human Mind" (1795), in *An Essay on the Principle of Population: Text, Sources and Background, Criticism*, ed. Philip Appleman (New York: Norton, 1976), 7–8.

6   Petersen, *Malthus*, 5–6.

7   Godwin, *Enquiry*, 62.

8   William Petersen, "The Malthus–Godwin Debate, Then and Now," *Demography* 8, no. 1 (1971): 13.

MODULE 4
THE AUTHOR'S CONTRIBUTION

KEY POINTS

- Malthus approached the question of human perfectibility by addressing population.

- Malthus's theory takes population growth as a given, inescapable trap that food production cannot overcome. The resulting checks on population will always restrict social progress.

- Malthus offered a new and systematic argument that social progress and growing populations are not mutually supportive, but at odds.

Author's Aims

Thomas Robert Malthus's original contribution to the question of "human perfectibility" was his population model. Around the time that Malthus was writing *An Essay on the Principle of Population*, most philosophers and political economists believed that a growing population caused prosperity, and that prosperity led to population growth. This classical position was based on the assumption that populations could only grow as large as the capacity of the land to feed them—an idea shared by Malthus, William Godwin,* and others. Scottish clergyman and economist Robert Wallace* interpreted this limit on population as indicating the importance of the "arts" of agriculture and fishing. He believed that as they improved, this would enable population to expand. It appears that Wallace considered "rendering the earth populous" and "making society flourish" as two mutually reinforcing processes.[1]

Interestingly, Malthus embraced nearly all the assumptions of the writers who preceded him on the topic of population, but he reached

> ❝ That the increase of population is necessarily limited by the means of subsistence,*
> That population does invariably increase when the means of subsistence increase, and,
> That the superior power of population is repressed, and the actual population kept equal to the means of subsistence, by misery and vice. ❞
>
> Thomas Robert Malthus, *An Essay on the Principle of Population*

a very different conclusion. Malthus agreed that population tended to grow until it reached the subsistence level*—the largest size that can be fed from the available land. But he claimed this trend would lead not to increases in agricultural yield through more efficient agricultural or fishing practices, but rather into a nearly inescapable trap. To the observations of these earlier writers, Malthus added one more: that population will always grow faster than the fertility of the land. This means that any attempt to increase the population by boosting the productivity of farming is hopeless in the long term.

The construction of this population model was, in many ways, just a device to address larger questions. Malthus was less interested in the ways that population dynamics functioned than in the *effect* of these dynamics on human societies. As such, in its most basic form, his *Essay* served as a kind of warning to hyper-optimists that forces beyond human control may restrict progress more than any political or economic factors.

Approach

Malthus's population principle used the notion of natural laws to challenge Godwin and the Marquis de Condorcet's* claims about "human perfectibility." In *Political Justice*, Godwin presented a political vision in which the removal of what he saw as outdated political institutions—including marriage and private property—led to greater prosperity.[2] Malthus countered by stating that such changes—most importantly the removal of marriage—would create "extraordinary encouragements to population." In other words, without being bound by a legally sanctioned marriage, people would give free rein to their sexual desires and produce more children, thus eventually undoing any social benefits. Note that in making this claim, Malthus relied on his rejection of the classical position that prosperity and population growth are interconnected.

For example, according to Robert Wallace's interpretations, Godwin's society, with no known constraints on population, would be very desirable. However, in the context of Malthus's population principle, some checks on population—such as famine and disease—will always constrain the well-being of a significant portion of society, regardless of political or economic institutions. The consequence of Malthus's *Essay* was to cast skepticism on the perfectibility argument.

Malthus's use of natural laws broadened the scope of the argument about humanity perfectibility, and the nature of his analysis evolved over the *Essay*'s six editions. While the first edition presented checks on population driven by natural law (misery and vice) as the dark, inescapable fate of all human societies, the subsequent editions gave humans an escape. That escape was moral restraint—namely controlling one's sexual urges and delaying having children. Malthus referred to those initial checks as "positive" (given by natural law), in contrast to the "preventive" check of moral restraint. By adding the element of moral restraint, Malthus directly connected his challenge of Godwin and Condorcet to more immediate political concerns in Britain at the time—most notably the debate surrounding the Poor Laws.* At issue was whether giving basic welfare relief to the poor was a viable solution to the problem of poverty. He claimed such relief would only lead the poor to have more children, thereby creating greater misery. During his life, Malthus remained a critic of the Poor Laws, and his population principle lent his critique greater weight.

Contribution in Context

Malthus wrote the *Essay*, his first major intellectual work, in relative isolation. In fact, he claimed to have initially drafted it "on the spur of the occasion, and from the few materials which were within my reach in a country situation."[3] As such, Malthus was not a member of any particular intellectual school of the time.

Some have speculated that Malthus drafted the *Essay* to try to defend the big landowners from the attacks of French Revolution* sympathizers. These critics see connections between Malthus's writings on political topics and his population principle. His endorsement of the Corn Laws,* which erected barriers to cereal imports, is seen to support these criticisms. Most political economists of Malthus's time opposed those trade laws designed to protect cereal producers as being, in effect, inefficient handouts to landed elites.[4] Malthus partly based his support of the Corn Laws on his belief that removing them would allow in cheaper cereals and thereby "encourage an increase of numbers" of the poor, which suggests that there may have been some link between his political thinking and his population principle.[5] But it seems likely that his use of the population principle emerged naturally from his debate with Godwin, rather than as a result of his political beliefs.

NOTES

1   Robert Wallace, *A Dissertation on the Numbers of Mankind in Ancient and Modern Times* (1753), in *An Essay on the Principle of Population: Text, Sources and Background, Criticism*, edited by Philip Appleman (New York: Norton, 1976), 4.

2   William Godwin, *Enquiry Concerning Political Justice and its Influence on Morals and Happiness* (London: G.G. and J. Robinson, 1798).

3   Thomas Robert Malthus, *An Essay on the Principle of Population*, ed. Donald Winch (Cambridge: Cambridge University Press, 1992), 7.

4   Donald Winch, *Malthus: A Very Short Introduction* (Oxford: Oxford University Press, 2013), 66.

5   Malthus, *Essay*, 164.

SECTION 2
IDEAS

MODULE 5
MAIN IDEAS

KEY POINTS

- Populations tend to grow at a geometric, or exponential, rate (1, 2, 4, 8, 16). Agricultural production—the primary source of food—grows at an arithmetic, or linear, rate (1, 2, 3, 4, 5).

- Eventually the demand for food will outstrip supply and cause the population to decrease.

- Malthus originally presented his population trap as a tragic inevitability, but later argued it could be overcome through "moral restraint."

Key Themes

Thomas Robert Malthus's *An Essay on the Principle of Population* presents a logical, well-thought-out argument about what limits human population growth. The argument makes three claims. First, that population is limited to the subsistence level*—the maximum number of people that can get the minimum necessary nourishment from the amount of food that is available. Second, that when unchecked, the population will always tend to grow faster than subsistence—the available food. Third, that the gap between the increase in the level of subsistence and the size of population must, in Malthus's words, "necessarily be checked by the periodical or constant action of moral restraint, vice, or misery."[1]

According to Malthus, two checks on population are always in place. One is positive (and by "positive," he meant determined by natural laws*). This is the "vice or misery" that inevitably accompanies overpopulation. Misery referred to famine and disease caused by

❝ If we treat Malthus as a practical demographer,* as someone attempting to explain actual population trends in order to propose measures designed to achieve more desirable rates of population growth, the significance of his ideas lay primarily in their defeat of a long-standing tradition which had automatically linked a large and growing population with economic progress and economic power. ❞

Donald Winch, *Malthus: A Very Short Introduction*

malnutrition. By "vice," Malthus meant practices widely viewed at the time as harmful and immoral, such as abortion, prostitution, and the spread of venereal disease. The other—and preferable—check is preventive: what he called "moral restraint." This meant, above all, abstaining from sex to delay having children, thereby slowing population growth.

Exploring the Ideas

To explain the positive check on population growth, Malthus used his training as a mathematician. He argued that unchecked population growth follows a geometric pattern, increasing according to the sequence 1, 2, 4, 8, 16 and so on. In contrast, the growth rate of land availability is linear, only increasing in the sequence 1, 2, 3, 4, 5, or until all land resources are used.[2] Because of this, he claimed, eventually population growth will always outpace the availability of food harvested from the land. Then, calamity will cause the population to revert back to the subsistence level.

This positive check generally raises the death rate through famine, malnourishment, or disease. It presents human societies with a choice: either suffer in misery and vice, or exercise what Malthus called "moral restraint."[3] Importantly, as Malthus explored this option, his language changed from that of logical scientist to that of someone arguing a particular point of view. He began using concepts of natural and moral evil to justify his claims. Taking the logic of his population model as given, Malthus argued that, one way or another, human population will be limited. The preventive checks that Malthus listed in the *Essay* were fewer in number than, but just as important as, the positive checks that occurred naturally. He dedicated the most time to "moral restraint" (i.e., sexual abstinence to avoid a large number of pregnancies), which he believed would come from a person's ability to "calculate distant consequences" of immediate actions.[4] He claimed that preventing population increase by choosing to have fewer children based on your ability to feed them was surely better than waiting for famine to reduce overpopulation. "It is better that this check should arrive from the foresight of the difficulties of attending a family, and the fear of dependent poverty, than from the actual presence of want and sickness."[5]

However, moral restraint is not the only preventive check Malthus identified in the *Essay*. He also believed that emigration could sometimes serve a similar purpose by reducing the population in the country people moved away from. But he said the effects would be only temporary, and the population would soon increase again.

Language and Expression

The *Essay* unfolds in four separate books, each organized into chapters. The first book presents the main argument, while the second and third books relate the argument to observations and statistical evidence from Europe and previous writing on the subject. The fourth book discusses the argument's implications for future human progress.

Malthus wrote the *Essay* in accessible language for the period, although some readers today may struggle with the formal language and some of the examples from that era. Beyond language that was specific to the time, the *Essay* is relatively free of jargon. This helps

Malthus's argument, because his main ideas about population trends are clearly explained in the text and are not complicated by too many difficult scientific terms.

NOTES

1   Thomas Robert Malthus, *An Essay on the Principle of Population*, ed. Donald Winch (Cambridge: Cambridge University Press, 1992), 56–67.

2   Malthus, *Essay*, 19.

3   Malthus, *Essay*, 207.

4   Malthus, *Essay*, 21.

5   Malthus, *Essay*, 207–8.

MODULE 6
SECONDARY IDEAS

KEY POINTS

- With the check on population as a given, any social policies, including the Poor Laws,* that tend to increase procreation will eventually lead to severe food shortages. Emigration, however, is a partial solution.

- Malthus's critique led to a reform of the Poor Laws designed to encourage recipients of aid to work.

- Malthus well-thought-out ideas influenced the Poor Laws, but his ideas—and influence—on emigration had less impact.

Other Themes

The most significant secondary idea in Malthus's *An Essay on the Principle of Population* is his critique of economic transfers to the poor—i.e., providing them with money or material help. The Poor Laws were the most important and controversial welfare program during Malthus's time. Considering his population model, Malthus stated that "though [these laws] may have alleviated a little of the intensity of individual misfortune, [they have] spread the evil over a much larger surface."[1]

Malthus was less hostile to other social policies and saw emigration as a possible remedy to some of the social pressures caused by population. He wrote: "When an opportunity as advantageous as emigration is offered, it is the fault of the people themselves if, instead of accepting it, they prefer a life of celibacy or extreme poverty in their home country."[2] He believed that emigration would transfer populations from places where population checks were strong to

> **❝** Though [the Poor Laws] may have alleviated a little of the intensity of individual misfortune, [they have] spread the evil over a much larger surface. **❞**
>
> Thomas Robert Malthus, *An Essay on the Principle of Population*

places where they were weaker, which would improve welfare. However, it is important to note that Malthus saw emigration as a "partial," not complete, solution to overpopulation,[3] since it would slow, but not reverse, the trend towards overpopulation.

Exploring the Ideas

Malthus's main argument against poor relief was that it would increase the population, which would in the longer term reduce welfare to a greater extent than the original benefit had increased it. He agreed that poor relief may "give a spur to productive industry." That was a claim proposed by its supporters based on the idea that the poor would use the relief to buy more goods, leading to increased production. But Malthus argued that this increase in productivity would be "more than counterbalanced by population," cancelling out any welfare gains as the available produce had to be spread across more people.[4]

Malthus suggested that any successful approach to poor relief would have to "raise the relative proportion between the price of labor and the price of provisions"—that is, it would increase wages, while not increasing prices in the same proportion.[5] However, according to his population principle, doing so would amount to increasing the ratio—the balance—of workers to agricultural output. He suggested that the idea of remedying this ratio by increasing agricultural productivity would amount to "setting the tortoise to catch the hare." (In this metaphor, the tortoise represents agricultural production and the hare population growth. As the hare is much faster than the tortoise, setting the tortoise to catch the hare would be hopeless.) He concluded that only decreasing the rate of population growth could realistically improve the plight of the poor,[6] and the most reliable path to achieving this was by advocating the use of "moral restraint" among the poor.[7]

Malthus was not entirely original in stating the potential negative effects of poor relief. In his 1786 *A Dissertation on the Poor Laws*, British physician and geologist Joseph Townsend* wrote that relief that has not been earned can lead people back into poverty: "It is universally found, that where bread can be obtained without care or labor, it leads through idleness and vice to poverty."[8]

Malthus advanced Townsend's theory by arguing that a transfer to the poor will have the effect of raising prices for all consumers, as more money chases after the same amount of goods. The result would again reduce overall welfare by lowering real wages.[9] Additionally, he suggested that poor relief would encourage the poor to marry earlier, undermining the "moral restraint" he considered the only appropriate escape from the population trap.

An interesting comparison can be made between Malthus's views on poor relief and emigration. In both cases, he places responsibility on the individual to make wise decisions—concerning poor relief, to raise the number of children that they know they can feed, and concerning emigration, to relocate to ease population pressure. This focus on the individual is a direct result of his population principle, which is based on the decisions of individuals as to how many children to have, and when.

Overlooked

Malthus's criticism of the Poor Laws was widely influential at the time, for both policymakers and scholars. His ideas were central to the Poor Law Amendment Act of 1834, which was designed to encourage work among those in the Poor Law system.[10] This sustained influence was thanks to both the clarity of his writing and strength of his ideas. Malthus was able to build a clear, logically consistent critique of welfare that stood apart from previous arguments based on moralizing alone. His writings on emigration are less notable, and it is not known whether his support of emigration policies influenced the government when it acted in 1826 to end laws that had added costs to such outward travel.

It should be noted that Malthus's discussion of "moral restraint" is an area where his religious views are revealed. One interesting example of that is his belief, based on St Paul's declarations on marriage in 1 Corinthians 7, that "when marriage does not interfere with higher duties, it is right; when it does, it is wrong." Malthus felt that adherence to what he called the "virtue" of the Christian religion was necessary to practice the "moral restraint" required to postpone marriage.[11]

The population principle gave Malthus's moral arguments a degree of originality, using the methods of scientific reasoning—something that was unique at the time. It is interesting to note that many of Malthus's discussions of moral issues emerged in later editions of the *Essay*. This was partly due to an ongoing debate between Malthus and some of his critics. But it also suggests that, as Malthus became more comfortable with the foundation of his argument—the population principle—he became more confident in discovering its extensions.

NOTES

1   Thomas Robert Malthus, *An Essay on the Principle of Population*, ed. Donald Winch (Cambridge: Cambridge University Press, 1992), 89.

2   Malthus, *Essay*, 85.

3   Malthus, *Essay*, 81.

4   Malthus, *Essay*, 90.

5   Malthus, *Essay*, 229.

6   Malthus, *Essay*, 230.

7   Malthus, *Essay*, 207.

8   Joseph Townsend, "A Dissertation on the Poor Laws" (1786), 11, accessed September 19, 2013, http://socserv2.socsci.mcmaster.ca/econ/ugcm/3ll3/townsend/poorlaw.html.

9   Malthus, *An Essay on the Principle of Population*, 98–9.

10 Ran Abramitzky and Fabio Braggion, "Malthusian and Neo-Malthusian Theories," in *The Oxford Encyclopedia of Economic History*, ed. Joel Mokyr (Oxford: Oxford University Press, 2003), 2.

11 Malthus, *Essay*, 221–2.

MODULE 7
ACHIEVEMENT

KEY POINTS

- Malthus was highly successful in constructing an argument against the claim that human societies can be perfected.

- Malthus used Isaac Newton's* scientific method* to construct a logical and systematic argument against popular idealistic views that he opposed.

- While the population principle was highly influential, the work itself was constructed with very little access to empirical data.

Assessing the Argument

Despite its central claim—that social and economic progress will inevitably be constrained by population—being called into question, Malthus's *An Essay on the Principle of Population* remains influential. That is partly due to the clarity and universality of his central idea. Malthus's population theory is abstract by design—he used mathematical examples to describe the relative rates at which population and agricultural production grow, as well as to justify the resulting checks on growth. With the exception of the preventive check (what he called the "moral restraint" of postponing pregnancies), he even suggested that his model could apply equally to plants and animals as to humans.[1]

Malthus was careful to note that the population checks he described would operate "with more or less force in every society," allowing for differences across time and space.[2] For example, he recognized that those checks would be more pronounced in England than in America, which at the time of the *Essay*'s publication was

> **❝** The main principle advanced is so incontrovertible
> that, if I had confined myself merely to general views,
> I could have entrenched myself in an impregnable
> fortress; and the work, in this form, would probably
> have had a much more masterly air. **❞**
>
> Thomas Robert Malthus, *An Essay on the Principle of Population*

rapidly expanding towards its western frontier, and opening huge amounts of land to farming for the first time.[3] Still, due to the wide gap between the geometric series that characterizes population growth (1, 2, 4, 8, 16) and the arithmetic series modeling the growth of food production (1, 2, 3, 4, 5), Malthus believed that his checks must exist to some degree in every society, regardless of its geographical situation or its legal or social institutions.

It is evidence of the success of this aspect of Malthus's argument that, as time has separated the *Essay* from its late-eighteenth-century context, the universal aspects of the text have gained greater prominence. Today, Malthus is almost solely associated with his population principle. While nineteenth-century readers immediately reacted to the *Essay* as a controversial piece about the use of social policy to increase welfare, twentieth-century writers have focused on the mechanics of Malthus's argument, particularly his mathematical analysis of population.[4]

Achievement in Context

When measuring the overall achievement of Malthus's *Essay*, we need to look at the evolution of the work over its six editions. The time and resources Malthus had available when he produced the first edition of the *Essay* severely limited the intellectual ambition of the project. He was unable to collect much statistical data to support his claims, and his knowledge of previous work on population was restricted. In fact, he conceded later that the population principle was developed only from the writings of David Hume,* Robert Wallace,* Adam Smith,* and Richard Price.*[5]

Malthus made some efforts to improve his limited access to empirical evidence. For example, between the publication of the first edition in 1798 and the second in 1803, he travelled to France and elsewhere in Europe to gather demographic* statistics to support his argument.[6] Furthermore, he gradually developed a richer understanding of previous work on population, and in the second edition he made reference to the work of Greek philosophers and French economists.[7] It is possible that, if Malthus had had access to more data, he would have seen that the population increases he saw in his lifetime were related to structural changes in food production due to new technologies. The same land could now support more people. So the population growth would not be turned around by hunger and disease, but would be permanent.

Although the *Essay* was significantly altered across its many editions—most notably between the first and second editions—the structure remained consistent. Malthus's argument sometimes wavers when he challenges his contemporaries such as William Godwin* or the Marquis de Condorcet;* however, the four books combine to form a coherent whole. They present his hypothesis, support it with factual evidence, relate it to competing hypotheses, and finally follow the implications of the hypothesis to its logical end. In this sense, the structure reflects the Newtonian scientific method* that was very influential at the time of publication.

Limitations

As an intellectual achievement, Malthus's population principle has had broad implications and wide-ranging applications. The continued importance of the *Essay* is partly due to the many intellectual creations it helped develop. Malthus's population model led directly to the

scientific study of demography, contributed to Charles Darwin's*
theory of evolution, and hinted at the law of diminishing returns* in
economics. This is the idea that when an input to production is
increased, if all other inputs remain constant, then the increase in
output will gradually diminish.

Malthus's role in guiding Darwin to his evolution principle is a
good example of the wide applicability of the *Essay*. Darwin credited
Malthus's population theory as providing him with the final insight to
fully develop his theory of evolution through natural selection. The
English naturalist Alfred Russel Wallace,* who developed the theory
of evolution independently from Darwin, also owed a debt to Malthus.
For Wallace, what was most important was recognizing the universality
of Malthus's population model, and—following on from this—
realizing that, in the competition between all species, "the inferior
would inevitably be killed off and the superior would remain."[8]

NOTES

1   Thomas Robert Malthus, *An Essay on the Principle of Population*, ed.
    Donald Winch (Cambridge: Cambridge University Press, 1992), 21.

2   Malthus, *Essay*, 21.

3   Malthus, *Essay*, 32–4.

4   Gregory Clark, *A Farewell to Alms: A Brief Economic History of the World*
    (Princeton, N.J.: Princeton University Press, 2007).

5   Malthus, *Essay*, 7–10.

6   Malthus, *Essay*, 7.

7   Malthus, *Essay*, 8.

8   Alfred Russel Wallace, *My Life: A Record of Events and Opinions* (New York:
    Dodd, Mead & Co., 1905), 361–2.

MODULE 8
PLACE IN THE AUTHOR'S WORK

KEY POINTS

- The population principle at the heart of the *Essay* is the centerpiece of Malthus's intellectual output.

- Throughout his career, Malthus also addressed broader political economy issues, such as the Poor Laws,* Corn Laws,* and poverty, but frequently based his arguments on aspects of his population principle.

- Even today, Malthus's population principle continues to influence political, economic, and agricultural debates about overpopulation.

Positioning

The majority of Thomas Robert Malthus's intellectual career was dedicated to the six editions of *An Essay on the Principle of Population*, published between 1798 and 1826. However, his ideas gradually evolved from his basic population theory to incorporate broader questions of political economy, and much of his later career was dedicated to subjects such as the Corn Laws and Poor Laws. Despite this wider reach (much of which was influenced by Malthus's long public discourse with British political economist David Ricardo*), Malthus continued to base many of his ideas around the population principle. Seen as a whole, the six editions of the *Essay* are the centerpiece of Malthus's intellectual output.

Apart from the *Essay*, Malthus's 1820 *Principles of Political Economy* is the most notable of his works. Somewhat ironically, Malthus based the *Principles* on the belief that "the science of political economy bears a nearer resemblance to the science of morals and politics than that of

> **❝** Many of those who approach political economy from a more secular perspective adopted Malthus's population principle as the foundation for their position on wages, the causes of poverty, and the need for fundamental changes in the Poor Law. **❞**
>
> Donald Winch, *Malthus: A Very Short Introduction*

mathematics."[1] Malthus believed that political economists like Ricardo were too quick to generalize the world into simple mathematical principles and too unwilling to recognize the "multicausal influences at work in the world."[2] It is evidence of Malthus's subtlety as a thinker that he simultaneously supported the scientific reasoning that underpinned his population principle and recognized the importance of multiple explanations for economic phenomena.

Integration

In the twentieth century, John Maynard Keynes,* an influential British economist who argued for government intervention to avoid depressions and promote stability, lamented the dominance of the Ricardian view in economics. "If only Malthus, instead of Ricardo, had been the parent stem from which nineteenth-century economics proceeded, what a much wiser and richer place the world would be today."[3]

In many ways, Malthus's population principle directly influenced his broader work in political economy. For example, one of his key interests as a political economist was the role of agriculture in the economy. In contrast to the dominant political economist of the time, Adam Smith,* the early Malthus believed agriculture was just as important as manufacturing for society's development, if not more so. In *The Wealth of Nations*, Smith stated that increases in industrial productivity allow the factory owners to accumulate enough money to allow for future investments. The result is economic growth, which causes increased demand for labor, higher wages, and lower prices for basic goods.[4] Malthus agreed that this capital accumulation could lead to greater general wealth through increased industrial production. But he felt that, without equally increasing agricultural production, further negative population checks—misery and vice—would continue to restrict human progress.

Later in his career, in the fifth and sixth editions of the *Essay* and in *Principles of Political Economy*, Malthus presented a more favorable view of manufacturing. This change may be evidence of his gradual acceptance of more widely held views on political economy. Interestingly, he based this later support of manufacturing partly on the belief that access to luxury goods made available by industry would encourage the hard work and prudence he felt would help liberate the masses from the population trap.

Significance

Despite later ventures into political economy and the issues of his day, Malthus's intellectual influence has been almost entirely connected to his population principle. In the nineteenth century, his model of population reached a wide audience, influencing politicians, scientists, and mathematicians, as well as political economists. More recently, his name continues to be attached to political, economic, and agricultural concerns about overpopulation.

Another legacy of Malthus's work—one he may not have anticipated during his lifetime—is his role in founding the field of demography, the statistical study of human populations. As Donald Winch wrote, Malthus "created the terrain over which demographic dispute continues to rage" by establishing a template for in-depth population research.[5] Although "Malthus has been criticized for paying insufficient attention to the quantitative evidence that was available to him, and for misinterpreting it when he did," his population model remains an important contribution to demographics.[6] For example, the idea of a connection between increases in food supply and inducements to population growth, while admittedly more complicated than Malthus's notion, remains a feature of demographic models.

NOTES

1 Donald Winch, *Malthus: A Very Short Introduction* (Oxford: Oxford University Press, 2013), 76.

2 Winch, *Malthus*, 76.

3 Winch, *Malthus*, 10.

4 Winch, *Malthus*, 58.

5 Winch, *Malthus*, 2.

6 Winch, *Malthus*, 95.

SECTION 3
IMPACT

MODULE 9
THE FIRST RESPONSES

KEY POINTS

- Immediate public reaction to the population principle was largely critical, due to the shocking implications of Malthus's idea. Conservatives, however, welcomed its implied attack on efforts to overturn the established order.

- Malthus said his critics were willfully ignoring the population checks (famine and disease) that would follow financial and material help to the poor.

- Many critics could not believe that the dismal conclusions of Malthus's Essay could have been put in place by God or nature.

Criticism

An Essay on the Principle of Population generated immediate critical reaction upon its publication in 1798, mostly aimed at the pessimistic view of society that seemed central to Thomas Robert Malthus's argument. For example, it is widely held that the term "dismal science"—used then to refer to the study of political economy and today in reference to economics—was coined by the Scottish philosopher Thomas Carlyle* upon reading Malthus's *Essay*.[1]

One particularly outspoken critic of Malthus was William Cobbett,* an English journalist known for his fiery, argumentative writing. While Cobbett initially embraced Malthus's *Essay*, he later changed his opinion, even at one time writing that he detested no man so much as Malthus.[2] A key feature of Cobbett's criticism was his belief that no natural laws could undermine other natural laws. Cobbett believed that love between people was the most fundamental

> ❝ Among other phenomena of the kind, I hailed
> the attack of Mr. Malthus. I believed that the *Essay
> on Population*, like other erroneous and exaggerated
> representations of things, would soon find its own level.
> In this I have been hitherto disappointed. ❞
>
> William Godwin,* "Of Population"

of natural laws, and thus he argued that Malthus's population principle, which detailed the harmful consequences that love could produce, was unnatural.[3] Cobbett's views were shared widely in the early nineteenth century, but did not leave a lasting mark on the general debate surrounding Malthus's writing.

A more influential contemporary critic of Malthus's work was William Godwin, whose own ideas were one of Malthus's primary targets. Particularly important was Godwin's suggestion that Malthus's population model did not consider changes in the nature of procreation caused by economic progress. Godwin believed that, as countries grew richer, sexual desire would be replaced with nobler pursuits, and that this would weaken the force of population growth. Ironically, Godwin's prediction has come true in some ways, although the low fertility in rich countries today is probably due more to the availability of birth control and the development of social safety nets than to the greater prudence Godwin imagined.

Meanwhile, some American writers, including political economist Daniel Raymond,* criticized Malthus's population principle on the grounds that poverty in England was not caused by overpopulation, as Malthus suggested, but by a "system of laws" that concentrated property rights in the hands of a few.[4] Raymond believed that a fairer distribution of property would solve the problem of inequality that Malthus had observed. In general, American political economists were skeptical of the concept of diminishing returns* implied by Malthus's population model. This was unsurprising, given the rapid population growth and rising agricultural productivity that were occurring side by side in America in the early nineteenth century.[5]

The final, and most aggressive, criticism directed at Malthus during his lifetime focused on his character. Malthus was accused of opposing all population growth, being a hired hand for the landed elite, and promoting the sickness and death of the poor.[6] Godwin accused Malthus's *Essay* of promoting "passiveness" towards the needy and a moral code "consisting principally of negatives."[7]

Responses

Malthus did not respond to many of these direct attacks during his lifetime; however, he did spend considerable time reacting to Godwin's critiques. In the second edition of the *Essay*, he responded to Godwin's idea that marriage and sexual behavior might change as society progresses. While Malthus remained convinced throughout his lifetime that "an attempt to execute [Godwin's political vision] would very greatly increase the quantity of vice and misery in society," he eventually agreed with Godwin's point that "moral restraint"—which Godwin termed "prudence"—was a feasible check on population.[8]

Malthus's later concession that humans can prevent "misery and vice" by delaying marriage and sexual behavior fundamentally altered the tone of his argument. While the original argument claimed humans were *inevitably* subject to nature's checks on population, allowing for moral restraint gave humans an escape. The long-term reception of Malthus's *Essay* changed considerably due to this alteration. As American scholar William Petersen wrote: "Over his lifetime ... Malthus moved from a biological to a sociological analysis, from principled pessimism to cautious optimism, and from a direct contradiction of Godwin to an accommodation to his main criticisms."[9]

As Petersen suggests, the addition of a preventive check on population allowed Malthus to focus not only on the rigid wall of population, but also on the social institutions—such as the Poor Laws*—that, in his view, undermined the effectiveness of moral restraint. While Malthus gradually moved towards Godwin's position over the course of his career, it would be an exaggeration to say they reached a consensus. Indeed, in Godwin's 1820 essay "Of Population," he labeled Malthus's population principle "erroneous and exaggerated."[10]

In response to the other criticisms—that he misunderstood nature's laws and showed no sympathy for the poor—Malthus often took the position of a detached social scientist merely reporting uncomfortable facts. In response to unnamed "popular orators and writers"—which may have referred to William Cobbett, among others—Malthus wrote: "Partly from ignorance, and partly from design, everything that could tend to enlighten the laboring classes as to the real nature of their situation … has been sedulously [i.e., 'with great effort and determination'] kept out of their view."[11]

Conflict and Consensus

Although Malthus's fundamentally negative text inspired many critical reactions, his detached tone in some ways helped the *Essay* achieve a better reception. His image as a bearer of unpleasant, but unavoidable, news has been attached to his name since the early nineteenth century. When his *Essay* was first published in 1798, it was immediately held up by conservatives to support their attacks on the French Revolution.* Conservatives rejected not only the Revolution's excesses, but also its progressive social policies. Irish political philosopher Edmund Burke,* one of the founders of modern conservatism, argued against the revolutionaries' introduction of relief for the poor in his *Reflections on the Revolution in France*.[12] Burke felt that society should be not be governed by new, abstract notions like universal rights, but rather by tradition. But Malthus's arguments were in some ways more persuasive because they were based on scientific reasoning, not on moral ideas. Using his population principle, Malthus claimed that improving the living standards of the poor, while intended to decrease economic inequality and suffering, would not be a permanent solution. Poor relief would, in his view, increase population, which would be followed by brutal checks on population: famine and disease.

NOTES

1   Robert J. Dixon, "Carlyle, Malthus, and Sismondi: The Origins of Carlyle's Dismal View of Political Economy," *History of Economics Review* 44 (2006): 32–8.

2   Charles H. Kegel, "William Cobbett and Malthusianism," *Journal of the History of Ideas* 19, no. 3 (1958): 350.

3   Kegel, "William Cobbett and Malthusianism," 350.

4   Daniel Raymond, *Thoughts on Political Economy* (Baltimore, MD: Fielding Lucas, 1820), 273.

5   George Johnson Cady, "The Early American Reaction to the Theory of Malthus," *Journal of Political Economy* 39, no. 5 (1931): 608.

6   Donald Winch, *Malthus: A Very Short Introduction* (Oxford: Oxford University Press, 2013), 5.

7   William Godwin, "Of Population: An Enquiry Concerning the Power of Increase in the Numbers of Mankind" (1820), in *An Essay on the Principle of Population: Text, Sources and Background, Criticism*, ed. Philip Appleman (New York: Norton, 1976), 143–4.

8   Thomas Robert Malthus, *An Essay on the Principle of Population*, ed. Donald Winch (Cambridge: Cambridge University Press, 1992), 69.

9   William Petersen, "The Malthus–Godwin Debate, Then and Now," *Demography* 8, no. 1 (1971): 19.

10 Godwin, "Of Population," 143.

11 Malthus, *Essay*, 257.

12 Edmund Burke, *Reflections on the Revolution in France, and on the Proceedings in Certain Societies in London Relative to that Event* (London: J. Dodsley, 1790).

MODULE 10
THE EVOLVING DEBATE

KEY POINTS

- Malthus's work has had a wide-ranging impact, from the development of the field of demography* to sub-fields in economics.

- Malthus's ideas have been attached to the iron law of wages* and the law of diminishing returns* as well as areas of economic history and endogenous growth theory.*

- Most scholars believe that the empirical predictions of Malthus's population principle no longer hold in most societies—at least not for now.

Uses and Problems

Thomas Robert Malthus's *An Essay on the Principle of Population* is uniquely positioned in the history of economic thought. His population principle was so persuasive at the time of publication that the view that was generally accepted up to that point—that population and prosperity were always positively linked—was cast into considerable doubt. An irony of Malthus's legacy is that the basic principles of his model began to change just as he wrote them down. Between 1750 and 1850, food production in Britain increased continuously, largely due to innovations such as crop rotations and the seed drill. This enabled population growth in ways of which Malthus was unaware.[1] In addition, the expansion of free trade, as argued for by Adam Smith,* opened up new areas of agricultural production and enabled Britain's escape from the Malthusian trap. With this in mind, Malthus's influence on economics has been limited since the nineteenth century, when technological change and international trade overturned many of his bolder predictions.

❝ The fact is that Malthus was right about *the whole of human history up until his own era.* **❞**
Paul Krugman,* "Malthus was Right!" *The New York Times*

During the nineteenth century, Malthus's ideas were attached to two key aspects of classical economic thought: the so-called iron law of wages and the law of diminishing returns. The iron law of wages, which is often attributed to David Ricardo,* states that wages will tend towards subsistence—the level at which workers earn just enough to buy the food they need to live—a view later adopted by Karl Marx.* Malthus did not make this claim, but his population principle seems to imply it. For example, assume that wages are above the subsistence level. According to Malthus, this will tend to increase population, driving up the supply of labor and thereby bringing wages back to subsistence. However, if wages are below subsistence, Malthus's population principle implies population will decrease until labor supply and demand meet at the subsistence level.

Another key economic descendant of Malthus's thinking is the law of diminishing returns. During Malthus's lifetime, the concept of diminishing returns related solely to limits on the fertility of the earth. The basic idea was that, as the use of land increases, the quality will diminish and lower average yields. However, after Malthus's death, American economist John Bates Clark* proposed a law of diminishing returns that applied to all production, not just agriculture. For example, suppose a firm is making clothes, and the two essential elements to produce the clothes are sewing machines and labor. If the number of sewing machines is fixed, the firm can increase production by adding labor—and thus perhaps by running the machines for longer. However, eventually the benefit of adding one more unit of labor will diminish because the machines will not be able to accommodate all the workers. It is interesting to note the similarity between this production system, in which adding one unit eventually undermines another, and Malthus's population principle, in which adding population lowers the average fertility of the land.

Schools of Thought

It would be difficult to fit Malthus's influence today into clearly defined schools of thought. Still, there exists a clear distinction between those concerned that population will outpace food production and, on the other hand, economists and food technologists who believe innovation will move fast enough to keep pace with population growth.

Since the nineteenth century, Malthus's influence has been largely outside economics, with exceptions being the fields of economic history and endogenous growth theory. This branch of economic theory is interested in explaining economic growth using factors already within the economy, rather than external agents such as technological advances, and here Malthusian ideas are still discussed. In economic history, Malthus's influence is primarily with historians who are interested in testing his population theory on pre-modern societies.

Ultimately, though, since the *Essay*'s predictions of crisis due to overpopulation have been mostly discarded, its long-term impact has been methodological. By constructing a model in which wages drive population trends, and population drives wages, Malthus produced an early example of economic equilibrium*—a state in which the forces in the economy are balanced. It is difficult to overstate the importance of this insight, as much of contemporary economics relies on equilibrium analysis related to Malthus's original population theory.

In Current Scholarship

Current advocates of the ideas contained in Malthus's *Essay* fall into two categories. Mainstream economists, such as Paul Krugman, believe that while Malthus's ideas held true for most of human history, recent and current innovations in food production can accommodate further resource limitations. On the other side are the neo-Malthusians, who believe that the rapid population growth projected for the near future will produce significant strains on resources and welfare.

Many economists are disciples of Malthus in the sense that they believe Malthus's population principle provides an accurate description of pre-industrial economies, or most economies in the world prior to 1800. However, they do not believe that his ideas can be applied to today's economies.[2] These critics argue that the technological advances created by industrialization—such as the seed drill, which distributes seeds evenly and at a depth inaccessible to birds—coupled with the spread of free trade, was enough to permanently break the historical relationship between population and the level of subsistence.[3] Thus, from the point of view of mainstream economists, the practical application of Malthusian thought today is to those economies that have yet to undergo the industrialization process—which includes most of Sub-Saharan Africa, parts of Asia and Latin America, and some areas in the developed world.[4]

In contrast, neo-Malthusians—a group that includes environmentalists such as Paul Ehrlich,* as well as a subset of researchers in organizations such as the World Bank* and the International Monetary Fund*—argue that technological innovation has merely postponed the inevitable population crisis described by Malthus's *Essay*.

The concerns of the neo-Malthusians are closely tied to concerns about global climate change and the unprecedented human impact on the environment due to industrial practices. Indeed, climate scientist Will Steffen suggested that the period from the Industrial Revolution to the present should be labeled the "Anthropocene" (meaning a geological age in which human activity has been the dominant influence on climate and environment) to indicate the relationship between human behavior and the global environment.[5] The availability of food—key to Malthus's ideas—is closely linked to climate. Research has shown that there is a negative relationship between crop yields and increases in global temperature that could have serious consequences for the future.[6] Another worrying example of the difficult relationship between human economic practices and food production is that man-made pesticides have been identified as a possible cause of the depletion of bee populations, or "colony collapse disorder.*" This, too, has an effect on future food production as the pollination of plants by bees is directly related to crop yields.[7]

Some scholars have attempted to find a middle ground between the mainstream economists and the neo-Malthusians. For example, ecological economists such as Robert Costanza[8] suggest a response to environmental challenges that includes a combination of technical innovation and sustainability—redesigning production and consumption so that they don't use up the earth's finite resources.

NOTES

1   Alexander Apostolides et al., "English Agricultural Output and Labour Productivity, 1250–1850: Some Preliminary Estimates," unpublished working paper (University of Warwick, 2008).

2   Gregory Clark, *A Farewell to Alms: A Brief Economic History of the World* (Princeton, N.J.: Princeton University Press, 2007).

3   Ran Abramitzky and Fabio Braggion, "Malthusian and Neo-Malthusian Theories," in *The Oxford Encyclopedia of Economic History*, ed. Joel Mokyr (Oxford: Oxford University Press, 2003), 8.

4   Paul Krugman, "Malthus was Right!" *The New York Times*, March 25, 2008.

5   Will Steffen et al., "The Anthropocene: Conceptual and Historical Perspectives," *Philosophical Transactions of the Royal Society* 369 (2011): 842–67.

6   Martin Parry, "The Implications of Climate Change for Crop Yields, Global Food Supply and Risk of Hunger," *International Crops Research Institute for the Semi-Arid Tropics eJournal* (2007), accessed October 1, 2013, www.icrisat.org/journal/SpecialProject/sp14.pdf.

7   Bryan Walsh, "The Trouble with Beekeeping in the Anthropocene,"
     Time, August 9, 2013, accessed October 1, 2013, http://science.time.
     com/2013/08/09/the-trouble-with-beekeeping-in-the-anthropocene/.

8   Robert Costanza et al., *An Introduction to Ecological Economics* (Boca
     Raton, FL: St. Lucie Press, 1997).

MODULE 11
IMPACT AND INFLUENCE TODAY

KEY POINTS

- The ideas in Malthus's *Essay* continue to demand that policy-makers and researchers take population seriously.

- Neo-Malthusians continue to apply Malthus's ideas to contemporary problems such as climate change.

- Despite its lasting influence many, including the majority of economists, view Malthus's warning as applicable exclusively to pre-1800s societies.

Position

Although it was written in a very different economic and political environment from today's, Thomas Robert Malthus's *An Essay on the Principle of Population* still challenges policy-makers and scholars to think about overpopulation. Much of the world has escaped the trap that Malthus proposed in 1798—living standards in America, Europe, and much of Asia far surpass those of late-eighteenth-century England. Pockets of the developing world today may sometimes face the Malthusian trade-off between population and prosperity. However, even where there is famine, it is typically due to war or local environmental degradation, and food is usually available on the market for those who can afford it. Yet with world population forecast to grow strongly for the rest of the century, the race between population and food supplies is on. Africa, the poorest continent, is expected to have increased its population by nearly 10 times between 1950 and 2050.[1]

Rapid economic growth and access to new production technologies have allowed contemporary wealthy nations to escape the Malthusian trap, and much of the intellectual challenge today

❝ The escape from hunger, poor health, and premature death which began in Malthus's age has not yet run its full course. **❞**
Robert Fogel, Nobel Prize Lecture (1993)

concerns whether those trends can continue in developing countries. World population is expected to grow to roughly eleven billion by 2100, which means that food production must increase substantially to accommodate more than four billion additional people.[2] Doing so will require the development of new agricultural biotechnology* (the development of practical applications using biological systems, such as genetically modified food) as well as the adoption of advanced farming techniques worldwide. The debate about this problem is mostly two-sided: On one side are those (including most economists) who believe technology will always progress fast enough to avoid a food-related calamity.[3] On the other are the neo-Malthusians who urge today's wealthy countries to consume less in order to better distribute the world's limited resources to the impoverished.[4]

As the economic historian Robert Fogel notes, the problem of overpopulation will probably never be wholly solved as long as human societies are dependent on agriculture for sustenance.[5] Fogel suggests that the prospects for fully entering a "post-Malthusian world"—where human opportunity is not limited by population—will depend on wealthy countries implementing policies that ensure environmental protection and the continual supply of innovation.[6]

The availability of demographic data today has enabled a much more sophisticated analysis of population changes than Malthus was able to perform. While he could access only basic population information from a few countries around the world, census data is now available from most countries, giving researchers an accurate picture of the global population. A significant portion of contemporary scholarship on the ideas Malthus championed is thus empirical—based on observation. For example, one paper uses population data from the World Bank* to document the Malthusian fact that, in poor countries with a high share of workers in agriculture, increased population tends to decrease living standards.[7]

Interaction

Malthus's *Essay* is relevant to the intellectual debate today between those who believe technology will advance fast enough to accommodate global population growth and those who don't. The main ideas in the *Essay* continue to challenge those who argue that technology will always outpace population pressure.

Economists who believe population growth may not be as damaging as the neo-Malthusians suggest can be roughly divided into in two categories. The first consists of economists who believe prices will adjust to encourage the kind of technological change that's needed to outpace population growth.[8] In short, their argument is that as food becomes scarce, prices will rise in accordance with standard market theory. This is based on the popular view among economists that market forces—supply and demand—tend to self-regulate allocation problems better than outside intervention. Higher prices have the effect of increasing farmers' margins (the difference between the sale price and cost of production) for each crop they sell, encouraging greater production. To boost production, some farmers—or crop scientists—will develop and implement new technologies—including advanced irrigation techniques, the use of better fertilizers and optimal crop schedules—that are then passed to other farmers. The severity of the change in prices dictates the extent of technological innovation, so that even a great strain on resources will be balanced out by equally great advances in farming technology.

Among the other Malthusian skeptics are followers of the Danish economist Ester Boserup,* who proposed in 1965 that a greater population might actually lead to a more efficient use of agricultural resources. Boserup's idea was that population growth could lead to agricultural "intensification"—the belief that more intense and frequent farming practices can improve yields.[9] As population density increases in agricultural areas, more workers would be available for jobs such as weeding, installing irrigation systems, and monitoring and harvesting crops—thereby boosting efficiency, while increasing total output.

The Continuing Debate

Despite the interesting findings of this kind of research, the contemporary response to Malthus's work remains something of an uncoordinated effort. Institutions such as the World Bank and the International Monetary Fund* have sponsored research and issued policy papers on the problems associated with overpopulation, and the United Nations* has a division devoted to population in its Department of Economic and Social Affairs. An example of this kind of work is the United Nations' *World Economic and Social Survey 2011*, which states that an increase in the "level of human activity is threatening to surpass the limits of the Earth's capacity" to both feed the population, and recycle the waste and pollution we produce without destroying the environment. Still, the academic community remains undecided on the topic of population, partly because of the scattered nature of the literature across the disciplines of economics, family planning, and environmental studies.[10]

There is some good news: most scientists believe the world's population—which doubled from 3.5 billion to seven billion in just the last half century—will peak sometime later this century and then remain stable or decline. But until then, global population is expected to increase by at least a couple of billion. Neo-Malthusian scholars worry that, especially with the disruptions likely to be caused by global warming, food production may not keep pace.

NOTES

1   David N. Weil and Joshua Wilde, "How Relevant is Malthus for Economic
    Development Today?" *American Economic Review* 99, no. 2 (2009): 255–60.

2   Erik Stokstad, "Will Malthus Continue to Be Wrong?" *Science* 309, no. 5731
    (2005): 102.

3   Ester Boserup, *The Conditions of Agricultural Growth: The Economics of
    Agrarian Change under Population Pressure* (New Brunswick, N.J.: Aldine
    Transaction, 2005).

4   David Price, "Of Population and False Hopes: Malthus and His Legacy,"
    Population and Environment: A Journal of Interdisciplinary Studies 19, no. 3
    (1998): 205–19; Paul R. Ehrlich, *The Population Bomb* (New York: Ballantine
    Books, 1968).

5   Robert W. Fogel, *The Relevance of Malthus for the Study of Mortality Today:
    Long-Run Influences on Health, Mortality, Labor Force Participation, and
    Population Growth* (Cambridge, MA: NBER Historical Working Paper Series No.
    54, 1994), 41.

6   Fogel, *The Relevance of Malthus*, 42.

7   Weil and Wilde, "How Relevant is Malthus?"

8   Justin Gillis, "Reverend Malthus and the Future of Food," *The New York Times*,
    June 6, 2011.

9   Boserup, *Conditions*, 15.

10 Monica Das Gupta et al., *Population, Poverty, and Sustainable Development: A
    Review of the Evidence* (Washington, D.C.: The World Bank, 2011).

MODULE 12
WHERE NEXT?

KEY POINTS

- Malthus's *Essay* will continue to be important as long as a significant portion of the world's population relies on agriculture for nourishment.

- The future importance of the text will depend on farming practices and yields worldwide.

- The work is seminal for its bold and controversial statement about population and, more generally, as a guide for how to apply systematic thinking to social problems.

Potential

When considering the future impact of *An Essay on the Principle of Population*, Thomas Robert Malthus's influence on the public's imagination should be distinguished from his influence as an economist. Despite key contributions to important economic concepts like the law of diminishing returns* and endogenous growth theory,* Malthus's influence on current economics is rather minimal. In fact, most economists believe that Malthus's population predictions are no longer valid, and very few graduate courses in economics teach Malthus.[1]

However, in the popular imagination, and in ongoing debates on global poverty, Malthus remains far more influential. That is largely due to the vocal nature of Malthus's disciples, but it is also related to the emerging problem of global climate change and whether the disruptions to food production that global warming could cause might lead to insufficient food supplies for a growing world population.[2]

> **❝** Malthus's *Essay* can be read as an applied treatise on the proper methods of reasoning in the moral or social sciences. **❞**
>
> Donald Winch, Introduction to *An Essay on the Principle of Population*

With those trends in mind, it is reasonable to believe that Malthus's ideas will continue to be used in the debate about the relationship between population and agricultural production.

Furthermore, Malthus's influence will probably depend on the policies followed in both advanced economies and especially underdeveloped countries to control population growth. If impoverished countries today—where Malthusian pressures still remain—find a way to maintain economic growth while increasing population, his *Essay* will eventually drift into obscurity. However, if the threat of misery created by competition over resources intensifies in these regions, his ideas will remain an important guidebook for dealing with the political economy of population. One response to the population problem is the use of population control,* which is a practice implemented by governments to reduce a population's fertility rate via a range of measures, including education, taxes, and access to contraceptives. China's one-child policy enacted in 1979, whereby the government fined families who had more than one child, is an extreme example. Another response is to set up programs that encourage girls to stay in school, which have been shown to lead to delayed marriage and lower fertility in poor countries.[3]

Future Directions

Malthus's core ideas are so entrenched in modern practices of demography* and population research that his influence is still widely felt by researchers and policy-makers. In one example of a study related to his work, researchers sponsored by the World Bank* showed that, in the Machakos district of Kenya, the population quadrupled between 1930 and 1990, despite the area being characterized by arid conditions.[4] Over that 60-year period, farmers in Machakos developed new irrigation techniques and introduced their crops to new markets—innovations that would not have been possible or necessary without rapid population growth. While these findings contradict some aspects of Malthus's population principle, the project is indicative of the kind of research that will continue to keep Malthus's ideas in circulation.

The United Nations Population Fund publishes new projections of global population growth every two years. But it is very hard to know with any certainty how many people will be living on the planet in the year 2100. It will depend on how much birthrates continue falling in the least developed nations—the countries where population is growing fastest. The UN says the most likely scenario is a global population of about 11 billion by the end of the century. But the world body says it could be as little as 7 billion and as much as 17 billion. Scientists will continue monitoring population growth closely, since, as the neo-Malthusians warn, the larger it gets, the greater the risk it will overstretch the earth's fragile resources and ability to produce enough food to feed everyone.

Summary

Malthus's *Essay* remains one of the most influential works of economics and demography ever written. And its influence remains despite many of his predictions being proven false by subsequent events. That influence can be attributed to the boldness of Malthus's initial argument, his clarity of writing, and the curiosity of thinkers from widely differing disciplines who have applied Malthus's ideas to their own field.

Perhaps most important, students should read the *Essay* as an exercise in applying scientific reasoning to social problems. Malthus's population principle was one of the first successful economic models. It begins with a set of assumptions and explicitly describes how those assumptions produce conclusions that you would not expect, nor necessarily predict. Students who are unfamiliar with that kind of reasoning should treat the *Essay* as an approachable introduction to the kind of thinking on which all of modern social science is based.

NOTES

1   Justin Gillis, "Reverend Malthus and the Future of Food," *The New York Times*, June 6, 2011.

2   Martin Parry, "The Implications of Climate Change for Crop Yields, Global Food Supply and Risk of Hunger," *International Crops Research Institute for the Semi-Arid Tropics eJournal* (2007), accessed October 1, 2013, www.icrisat.org/journal/SpecialProject/sp14.pdf.

3   Steve Connor, "Educate Girls to Stop Population Soaring," *Independent*, December 4, 2008.

4   Mary Tiffen et al., *More People, Less Erosion: Environmental Recovery in Kenya* (Chichester: John Wiley & Sons, 1994).

GLOSSARY

GLOSSARY OF TERMS

Anarchism: a political philosophy based on the principle of no government. In the place of the state, anarchists support volunteerism and self-governance.

Biotechnology: the development of practical applications using biological systems; a common use of biotechnology in agriculture is the development of genetically modified food.

Colony collapse disorder: a problem first reported by beekeepers in 2006, in which adult honey bees die or abandon their hives. Many crops will not grow without honey bees, including apples, cucumbers, broccoli, onions, pumpkins, carrots, avocados, and almonds.

Corn Laws: protectionist trade laws in England in effect between 1815 and 1846, designed to protect cereal producers.

Demography: the statistical study of human populations.

Diminishing marginal utility: an economic concept that states that, as an agent consumes more, the utility derived from each additional unit will gradually decrease, although total utility may increase.

Dissenting academies: English educational institutions in the seventeenth, eighteenth and nineteenth centuries that gave Protestant students dissenting from the Church of England (who were usually excluded from traditional institutions such as the universities of Oxford and Cambridge) access to higher education.

Economic equilibrium: a state in which the forces in the economy are balanced; the most common example of economic equilibrium is a market in which the price exactly matches the point where supply and demand for a product intersect.

Endogenous growth theory: a branch of economic theory that tries to explain the process of economic growth using factors in the economy, such as investments in human capital and innovation, rather than external factors, such as technical progress, employed in traditional exogenous growth models.

Enlightenment: a European intellectual movement of the late seventeenth and eighteenth centuries emphasizing reason and individualism rather than tradition. It challenged the traditional authority of the Catholic Church and the continent's monarchies.

French Revolution: a period of radical social upheaval in France between 1789 and 1799 that marked the end of monarchy in France and the emergence of democratic rule.

International Monetary Fund (IMF): an organization of 188 countries, based in Washington, D.C., that promotes global financial stability. It lends money to heavily indebted countries when no one else will.

Invisible hand: an economic concept and metaphor that first appeared in Adam Smith's *The Wealth of Nations*. It refers to aspects of markets that are self-regulating. For example, the phrase may refer to the idea that prices in a market tend to adjust to shocks without outside interference.

Iron law of wages: a concept that states that wages will tend towards the level of subsistence—a view that was later adopted by Marx.

Law of diminishing returns: an economic concept that states that, when an input to production is increased, holding other inputs constant, the increase in output will gradually diminish.

Natural laws: rules that govern the natural world and human society, that are determined by nature, and so are universal. Natural laws are often contrasted with laws made by a particular society or state.

Newtonian scientific method: a method that consists of four rules for scientific reasoning: all proposed causes of natural phenomena must be observable, the same effects must be assigned to the same causes, proposed qualities of objects must be seen as universal, and theories must be considered true until proven otherwise.

Poor Laws: a set of social welfare programs in England that provided basic relief to the very poor. The Poor Law system persisted in England until the mid-twentieth century.

Population control: the practice of lowering the fertility rate of a population by a range of measures, including education, taxation, and access to contraceptives.

Subsistence level: defined as the minimum amount of food needed to survive.

United Nations: an organization of 193 countries, established in 1945 to promote world peace and cooperation among nations.

Utopianism: a political philosophy based on the idea that society can be perfected if rid of irrational institutions. In the late eighteenth century, concurrent with the French Revolution, Godwin and Condorcet were the most prominent representatives of this position.

World Bank: The International Bank for Reconstruction and Development, known as the World Bank, is an organization of 188 countries, based in Washington, D.C., that assists low- and middle-income countries to reduce poverty and develop their economies.

PEOPLE MENTIONED IN THE TEXT

Ester Boserup (1910–99) was a Danish economist who worked in the field of agricultural economics.

Edmund Burke (1729–97) was an Irish political philosopher and statesman known for his work *Reflections on the Revolution in France* (1790). He is considered one of the intellectual fathers of modern conservatism.

Thomas Carlyle (1795–1881) was a Scottish philosopher known for his social criticism and for historical works such as *The French Revolution: A History* (1837).

John Bates Clark (1847–1938) was an American economist known as a pioneer of marginal utility theory.

William Cobbett (1763–1835) was an English writer and journalist known for his role as a champion of rural life in the midst of the Industrial Revolution.

Marquis de Condorcet (1743–94) was a French philosopher and mathematician known for his essay "Sketch for a Historical Picture of the Progress of the Human Mind" (1795), as well as his early contributions to political science.

Charles Darwin (1809–82) was a British naturalist whose work *On the Origin of Species* first developed the theory of evolution caused by natural selection.

Paul Ehrlich (born 1932) is an American biologist best known for his outspoken views on overpopulation, as expressed in his book *The Population Bomb* (1968).

William Godwin (1756–1836) was a British philosopher whose work *Enquiry Concerning Political Justice and Its Influence on Morals and Happiness* is considered a founding text in the philosophy of anarchism, which advocates non-hierarchical individual freedom over state control.

David Hume (1711–76) was a highly influential Scottish philosopher and political economist known for his works *A Treatise on Human Nature* (1739), *Enquiries Concerning Human Understanding* (1748), and *Concerning the Principles of Morals* (1751).

John Maynard Keynes (1883–1946) was a British economist known for his work on business cycles and macroeconomics, and the intellectual founder of Keynesian economics.

Paul Krugman (born 1953) is an American economist whose work on international trade earned him a Nobel Prize in 2008. He is also widely known as a commentator on politics and economics for *The New York Times*.

Karl Marx (1818–83) was a German philosopher whose works *Capital* and *The Communist Manifesto* form the intellectual basis for communism.

Isaac Newton (1642–1727) was an English physicist and mathematician considered one of the most influential scientists of all time, whose scientific method emphasized constructing testable hypotheses and testing them with experimental data.

Richard Price (1723–91) was a Welsh moral philosopher and nonconformist preacher who promoted radical, liberal, and republican causes. He also wrote pamphlets about demography and finance.

Daniel Raymond (1786–1849) was an American economist who wrote *Thoughts on Political Economy* (1820) and *The Elements of Political Economy* (1823). He is considered to be the first important American economist.

David Ricardo (1772–1823) was a British political economist who developed the theory of comparative advantage. He is known for his systematic and reductive approach to economics, in contrast to the more holistic perspective of Malthus.

Jean-Jacques Rousseau (1712–78) was a Genevan philosopher known for his works *Discourses on the Origin of Inequality* (1755) and *On the Social Contract* (1762), as well as his influence on the French Revolution.

Adam Smith (1723–90) was a Scottish philosopher and political economist best known for his works *The Theory of Moral Sentiments* (1759) and *An Enquiry into the Nature and Causes of the Wealth of Nations* (1776). The latter is widely considered to be the first modern work of economics.

Joseph Townsend (1739–1816) was a British physician and geologist whose most notable work was the treatise *A Dissertation on the Poor Laws* (1786), in which he provided one of the first critiques of poor relief.

Alfred Russel Wallace (1823–1913) was an English naturalist known for developing the theory of evolution through natural selection independently of Charles Darwin.

Robert Wallace (1697–1771) was a Scottish clergyman and economist whose work *A Dissertation on the Numbers of Mankind in Ancient and Modern Times* (1753) was one of Malthus's primary influences.

WORKS CITED

WORKS CITED

Abramitzky, Ran, and Fabio Braggion. "Malthusian and Neo-Malthusian Theories." In *The Oxford Encyclopedia of Economic History*, edited by Joel Mokyr. Oxford: Oxford University Press, 2003.

Apostolides, Alexander, Stephen Broadberry, Bruce Campbell, Mark Overton, and Bas van Leeuwen. "English Agricultural Output and Labour Productivity, 1250–1850: Some Preliminary Estimates." Unpublished working paper. University of Warwick, 2008.

Barlow, Nora, ed. *The Autobiography of Charles Darwin: 1809–1882*. New York: Collins, 1958.

Boserup, Ester. *The Conditions of Agricultural Growth: The Economics of Agrarian Change under Population Pressure*. New Brunswick, N.J.: Aldine Transaction, 2005.

Burke, Edmund. *Reflections on the Revolution in France, and on the Proceedings in Certain Societies in London Relative to that Event*. London: J. Dodsley, 1790.

Cady, George Johnson. "The Early American Reaction to the Theory of Malthus." *Journal of Political Economy* 39, no. 5 (1931): 601–20.

Clark, Gregory. *A Farewell to Alms: A Brief Economic History of the World*. Princeton, N.J.: Princeton University Press, 2007.

Condorcet, Marquis de. "Sketch for a Historical Picture of the Progress of the Human Mind" (1795). In *An Essay on the Principle of Population: Text, Sources and Background, Criticism*, edited by Philip Appleman, 7–8. New York: Norton, 1976.

Connor, Steve. "Educate Girls to Stop Population Soaring." *Independent*, December 4, 2008.

Costanza, Robert, John H. Cumberland, Herman Daly, Robert Goodland, and Richard B. Norgaard. *An Introduction to Ecological Economics*. Boca Raton, FL: St. Lucie Press, 1997.

Das Gupta, Monica, John Bongaarts, and John Cleland. *Population, Poverty, and Sustainable Development: A Review of the Evidence*. Washington, D.C.: The World Bank, 2011.

Dixon, Robert J. "Carlyle, Malthus, and Sismondi: The Origins of Carlyle's Dismal View of Political Economy." *History of Economics Review* 44 (2006): 32–8.

Ehrlich, Paul R. *The Population Bomb*. New York: Ballantine Books, 1968.

Ehrlich, Paul R., and Anne H. Ehrlich. "Can a Collapse of Global Civilization Be Avoided?" *Proceedings of the Royal Society: Biological Sciences* 280, no. 1754 (2013). Accessed February 2, 2015. doi:10.1098/rspb.2012.2845.

Fogel, Robert W. "The Relevance of Malthus for the Study of Mortality Today: Long-Run Influences on Health, Mortality, Labor Force Participation, and Population Growth." Cambridge, MA: NBER Historical Working Paper Series no. 54, 1994.

Gillis, Justin. "Reverend Malthus and the Future of Food." *The New York Times*, June 6, 2011.

Godwin, William. *Enquiry Concerning Political Justice and Its Influence on Morals and Happiness*. London: G.G. and J. Robinson, 1798.

"Of Population: An Enquiry Concerning the Power of Increase in the Numbers of Mankind" (1820). In *An Essay on the Principle of Population: Text, Sources and Background, Criticism*, edited by Philip Appleman, 143–4. New York: Norton, 1976.

Hume, David. "Of the Populousness of Ancient Nations" (1752). In *An Essay on the Principle of Population: Text, Sources and Background, Criticism*, edited by Philip Appleman, 3. New York: Norton, 1976.

Kegel, Charles H. "William Cobbett and Malthusianism." *Journal of the History of Ideas* 19, no. 3 (1958): 348–62.

Krugman, Paul. "Malthus was Right!" *The New York Times*, March 25, 2008.

Malthus, Thomas Robert. *An Essay on the Principle of Population*, edited by Donald Winch. Cambridge: Cambridge University Press, 1992.

Marx, Karl. "Capital—Footnote to Part VII, Chapter 25, Section I." In *An Essay on the Principle of Population: Text, Sources and Background, Criticism*, edited by Philip Appleman, 159. New York: Norton, 1976.

Parry, Martin. "The Implications of Climate Change for Crop Yields, Global Food Supply and Risk of Hunger." *International Crops Research Institute for the Semi-Arid Tropics eJournal* (2007). Accessed October 1, 2013. www.icrisat.org/journal/SpecialProject/sp14.pdf.

Petersen, William. *Malthus: Founder of Modern Demography*. New Brunswick, N.J.: Transaction Publishers, 1999.

"The Malthus–Godwin Debate, Then and Now." *Demography* 8, no. 1 (1971): 13–26.

Price, David. "Of Population and False Hopes: Malthus and His Legacy." *Population and Environment: A Journal of Interdisciplinary Studies* 19, no. 3 (1998): 205–19.

Raymond, Daniel. *Thoughts on Political Economy*. Baltimore, MD: Fielding Lucas, 1820.

Steffen, Will, Jacques Grinevald, Paul Crutzen, and John McNeill. "The Anthropocene: Conceptual and Historical Perspectives." *Philosophical Transactions of the Royal Society* 369 (2011): 842–67.

Stokstad, Erik. "Will Malthus Continue to Be Wrong?" *Science* 309, no. 5731 (2005): 102.

"The Revenge of Malthus." *The Economist*, August 6, 2011.

Tiffen, Mary, Michael Mortimore, and Francis Gichuki. *More People, Less Erosion: Environmental Recovery in Kenya*. Chichester: John Wiley & Sons, 1994.

Townsend, Joseph. "A Dissertation on the Poor Laws" (1786). Accessed September 19, 2013. http://socserv2.socsci.mcmaster.ca/econ/ugcm/3ll3/townsend/poorlaw.html.

United Nations Economic and Social Affairs. *World Economic and Social Survey 2011: The Great Green Technological Transformation* (2011). Accessed February 2, 2015. www.un.org/en/development/desa/policy/wess/wess_current/2011wess.pdf

Wallace, Alfred Russel. *My Life: A Record of Events and Opinions*. New York: Dodd, Mead & Co., 1905.

Wallace, Robert. *A Dissertation on the Numbers of Mankind in Ancient and Modern Times* (1753). In *An Essay on the Principle of Population: Text, Sources and Background, Criticism*, edited by Philip Appleman, 4. New York: Norton, 1976.

Walsh, Bryan. "The Trouble with Beekeeping in the Anthropocene." *Time*, August 9, 2013. Accessed October 1, 2013. http://science.time.com/2013/08/09/the-trouble-with-beekeeping-in-the-anthropocene/.

Weil, David N., and Joshua Wilde. "How Relevant is Malthus for Economic Development Today?" *American Economic Review* 99, no. 2 (2009): 255–60.

Winch, Donald. *Malthus: A Very Short Introduction*. Oxford: Oxford University Press, 2013.

THE MACAT LIBRARY
BY DISCIPLINE

AFRICANA STUDIES

Chinua Achebe's *An Image of Africa: Racism in Conrad's Heart of Darkness*
W. E. B. Du Bois's *The Souls of Black Folk*
Zora Neale Huston's *Characteristics of Negro Expression*
Martin Luther King Jr's *Why We Can't Wait*
Toni Morrison's *Playing in the Dark: Whiteness in the American Literary Imagination*

ANTHROPOLOGY

Arjun Appadurai's *Modernity at Large: Cultural Dimensions of Globalisation*
Philippe Ariès's *Centuries of Childhood*
Franz Boas's *Race, Language and Culture*
Kim Chan & Renée Mauborgne's *Blue Ocean Strategy*
Jared Diamond's *Guns, Germs & Steel: the Fate of Human Societies*
Jared Diamond's *Collapse: How Societies Choose to Fail or Survive*
E. E. Evans-Pritchard's *Witchcraft, Oracles and Magic Among the Azande*
James Ferguson's *The Anti-Politics Machine*
Clifford Geertz's *The Interpretation of Cultures*
David Graeber's *Debt: the First 5000 Years*
Karen Ho's *Liquidated: An Ethnography of Wall Street*
Geert Hofstede's *Culture's Consequences: Comparing Values, Behaviors, Institutes and Organizations across Nations*
Claude Lévi-Strauss's *Structural Anthropology*
Jay Macleod's *Ain't No Makin' It: Aspirations and Attainment in a Low-Income Neighborhood*
Saba Mahmood's *The Politics of Piety: The Islamic Revival and the Feminist Subject*
Marcel Mauss's *The Gift*

BUSINESS

Jean Lave & Etienne Wenger's *Situated Learning*
Theodore Levitt's *Marketing Myopia*
Burton G. Malkiel's *A Random Walk Down Wall Street*
Douglas McGregor's *The Human Side of Enterprise*
Michael Porter's *Competitive Strategy: Creating and Sustaining Superior Performance*
John Kotter's *Leading Change*
C. K. Prahalad & Gary Hamel's *The Core Competence of the Corporation*

CRIMINOLOGY

Michelle Alexander's *The New Jim Crow: Mass Incarceration in the Age of Colorblindness*
Michael R. Gottfredson & Travis Hirschi's *A General Theory of Crime*
Richard Herrnstein & Charles A. Murray's *The Bell Curve: Intelligence and Class Structure in American Life*
Elizabeth Loftus's *Eyewitness Testimony*
Jay Macleod's *Ain't No Makin' It: Aspirations and Attainment in a Low-Income Neighborhood*
Philip Zimbardo's *The Lucifer Effect*

ECONOMICS

Janet Abu-Lughod's *Before European Hegemony*
Ha-Joon Chang's *Kicking Away the Ladder*
David Brion Davis's *The Problem of Slavery in the Age of Revolution*
Milton Friedman's *The Role of Monetary Policy*
Milton Friedman's *Capitalism and Freedom*
David Graeber's *Debt: the First 5000 Years*
Friedrich Hayek's *The Road to Serfdom*
Karen Ho's *Liquidated: An Ethnography of Wall Street*

John Maynard Keynes's *The General Theory of Employment, Interest and Money*
Charles P. Kindleberger's *Manias, Panics and Crashes*
Robert Lucas's *Why Doesn't Capital Flow from Rich to Poor Countries?*
Burton G. Malkiel's *A Random Walk Down Wall Street*
Thomas Robert Malthus's *An Essay on the Principle of Population*
Karl Marx's *Capital*
Thomas Piketty's *Capital in the Twenty-First Century*
Amartya Sen's *Development as Freedom*
Adam Smith's *The Wealth of Nations*
Nassim Nicholas Taleb's *The Black Swan: The Impact of the Highly Improbable*
Amos Tversky's & Daniel Kahneman's *Judgment under Uncertainty: Heuristics and Biases*
Mahbub Ul Haq's *Reflections on Human Development*
Max Weber's *The Protestant Ethic and the Spirit of Capitalism*

FEMINISM AND GENDER STUDIES

Judith Butler's *Gender Trouble*
Simone De Beauvoir's *The Second Sex*
Michel Foucault's *History of Sexuality*
Betty Friedan's *The Feminine Mystique*
Saba Mahmood's *The Politics of Piety: The Islamic Revival and the Feminist Subject*
Joan Wallach Scott's *Gender and the Politics of History*
Mary Wollstonecraft's *A Vindication of the Rights of Woman*
Virginia Woolf's *A Room of One's Own*

GEOGRAPHY

The Brundtland Report's *Our Common Future*
Rachel Carson's *Silent Spring*
Charles Darwin's *On the Origin of Species*
James Ferguson's *The Anti-Politics Machine*
Jane Jacobs's *The Death and Life of Great American Cities*
James Lovelock's *Gaia: A New Look at Life on Earth*
Amartya Sen's *Development as Freedom*
Mathis Wackernagel & William Rees's *Our Ecological Footprint*

HISTORY

Janet Abu-Lughod's *Before European Hegemony*
Benedict Anderson's *Imagined Communities*
Bernard Bailyn's *The Ideological Origins of the American Revolution*
Hanna Batatu's *The Old Social Classes And The Revolutionary Movements Of Iraq*
Christopher Browning's *Ordinary Men: Reserve Police Batallion 101 and the Final Solution in Poland*
Edmund Burke's *Reflections on the Revolution in France*
William Cronon's *Nature's Metropolis: Chicago And The Great West*
Alfred W. Crosby's *The Columbian Exchange*
Hamid Dabashi's *Iran: A People Interrupted*
David Brion Davis's *The Problem of Slavery in the Age of Revolution*
Nathalie Zemon Davis's *The Return of Martin Guerre*
Jared Diamond's *Guns, Germs & Steel: the Fate of Human Societies*
Frank Dikotter's *Mao's Great Famine*
John W Dower's *War Without Mercy: Race And Power In The Pacific War*
W. E. B. Du Bois's *The Souls of Black Folk*
Richard J. Evans's *In Defence of History*
Lucien Febvre's *The Problem of Unbelief in the 16th Century*
Sheila Fitzpatrick's *Everyday Stalinism*

Eric Foner's *Reconstruction: America's Unfinished Revolution, 1863-1877*
Michel Foucault's *Discipline and Punish*
Michel Foucault's *History of Sexuality*
Francis Fukuyama's *The End of History and the Last Man*
John Lewis Gaddis's *We Now Know: Rethinking Cold War History*
Ernest Gellner's *Nations and Nationalism*
Eugene Genovese's *Roll, Jordan, Roll: The World the Slaves Made*
Carlo Ginzburg's *The Night Battles*
Daniel Goldhagen's *Hitler's Willing Executioners*
Jack Goldstone's *Revolution and Rebellion in the Early Modern World*
Antonio Gramsci's *The Prison Notebooks*
Alexander Hamilton, John Jay & James Madison's *The Federalist Papers*
Christopher Hill's *The World Turned Upside Down*
Carole Hillenbrand's *The Crusades: Islamic Perspectives*
Thomas Hobbes's *Leviathan*
Eric Hobsbawm's *The Age Of Revolution*
John A. Hobson's *Imperialism: A Study*
Albert Hourani's *History of the Arab Peoples*
Samuel P. Huntington's *The Clash of Civilizations and the Remaking of World Order*
C. L. R. James's *The Black Jacobins*
Tony Judt's *Postwar: A History of Europe Since 1945*
Ernst Kantorowicz's *The King's Two Bodies: A Study in Medieval Political Theology*
Paul Kennedy's *The Rise and Fall of the Great Powers*
Ian Kershaw's *The "Hitler Myth": Image and Reality in the Third Reich*
John Maynard Keynes's *The General Theory of Employment, Interest and Money*
Charles P. Kindleberger's *Manias, Panics and Crashes*
Martin Luther King Jr's *Why We Can't Wait*
Henry Kissinger's *World Order: Reflections on the Character of Nations and the Course of History*
Thomas Kuhn's *The Structure of Scientific Revolutions*
Georges Lefebvre's *The Coming of the French Revolution*
John Locke's *Two Treatises of Government*
Niccolò Machiavelli's *The Prince*
Thomas Robert Malthus's *An Essay on the Principle of Population*
Mahmood Mamdani's *Citizen and Subject: Contemporary Africa And The Legacy Of Late Colonialism*
Karl Marx's *Capital*
Stanley Milgram's *Obedience to Authority*
John Stuart Mill's *On Liberty*
Thomas Paine's *Common Sense*
Thomas Paine's *Rights of Man*
Geoffrey Parker's *Global Crisis: War, Climate Change and Catastrophe in the Seventeenth Century*
Jonathan Riley-Smith's *The First Crusade and the Idea of Crusading*
Jean-Jacques Rousseau's *The Social Contract*
Joan Wallach Scott's *Gender and the Politics of History*
Theda Skocpol's *States and Social Revolutions*
Adam Smith's *The Wealth of Nations*
Timothy Snyder's *Bloodlands: Europe Between Hitler and Stalin*
Sun Tzu's *The Art of War*
Keith Thomas's *Religion and the Decline of Magic*
Thucydides's *The History of the Peloponnesian War*
Frederick Jackson Turner's *The Significance of the Frontier in American History*
Odd Arne Westad's *The Global Cold War: Third World Interventions And The Making Of Our Times*

The Macat Library By Discipline

LITERATURE

Chinua Achebe's *An Image of Africa: Racism in Conrad's Heart of Darkness*
Roland Barthes's *Mythologies*
Homi K. Bhabha's *The Location of Culture*
Judith Butler's *Gender Trouble*
Simone De Beauvoir's *The Second Sex*
Ferdinand De Saussure's *Course in General Linguistics*
T. S. Eliot's *The Sacred Wood: Essays on Poetry and Criticism*
Zora Neale Huston's *Characteristics of Negro Expression*
Toni Morrison's *Playing in the Dark: Whiteness in the American Literary Imagination*
Edward Said's *Orientalism*
Gayatri Chakravorty Spivak's *Can the Subaltern Speak?*
Mary Wollstonecraft's *A Vindication of the Rights of Women*
Virginia Woolf's *A Room of One's Own*

PHILOSOPHY

Elizabeth Anscombe's *Modern Moral Philosophy*
Hannah Arendt's *The Human Condition*
Aristotle's *Metaphysics*
Aristotle's *Nicomachean Ethics*
Edmund Gettier's *Is Justified True Belief Knowledge?*
Georg Wilhelm Friedrich Hegel's *Phenomenology of Spirit*
David Hume's *Dialogues Concerning Natural Religion*
David Hume's *The Enquiry for Human Understanding*
Immanuel Kant's *Religion within the Boundaries of Mere Reason*
Immanuel Kant's *Critique of Pure Reason*
Søren Kierkegaard's *The Sickness Unto Death*
Søren Kierkegaard's *Fear and Trembling*
C. S. Lewis's *The Abolition of Man*
Alasdair MacIntyre's *After Virtue*
Marcus Aurelius's *Meditations*
Friedrich Nietzsche's *On the Genealogy of Morality*
Friedrich Nietzsche's *Beyond Good and Evil*
Plato's *Republic*
Plato's *Symposium*
Jean-Jacques Rousseau's *The Social Contract*
Gilbert Ryle's *The Concept of Mind*
Baruch Spinoza's *Ethics*
Sun Tzu's *The Art of War*
Ludwig Wittgenstein's *Philosophical Investigations*

POLITICS

Benedict Anderson's *Imagined Communities*
Aristotle's *Politics*
Bernard Bailyn's *The Ideological Origins of the American Revolution*
Edmund Burke's *Reflections on the Revolution in France*
John C. Calhoun's *A Disquisition on Government*
Ha-Joon Chang's *Kicking Away the Ladder*
Hamid Dabashi's *Iran: A People Interrupted*
Hamid Dabashi's *Theology of Discontent: The Ideological Foundation of the Islamic Revolution in Iran*
Robert Dahl's *Democracy and its Critics*
Robert Dahl's *Who Governs?*
David Brion Davis's *The Problem of Slavery in the Age of Revolution*

Alexis De Tocqueville's *Democracy in America*
James Ferguson's *The Anti-Politics Machine*
Frank Dikotter's *Mao's Great Famine*
Sheila Fitzpatrick's *Everyday Stalinism*
Eric Foner's *Reconstruction: America's Unfinished Revolution, 1863-1877*
Milton Friedman's *Capitalism and Freedom*
Francis Fukuyama's *The End of History and the Last Man*
John Lewis Gaddis's *We Now Know: Rethinking Cold War History*
Ernest Gellner's *Nations and Nationalism*
David Graeber's *Debt: the First 5000 Years*
Antonio Gramsci's *The Prison Notebooks*
Alexander Hamilton, John Jay & James Madison's *The Federalist Papers*
Friedrich Hayek's *The Road to Serfdom*
Christopher Hill's *The World Turned Upside Down*
Thomas Hobbes's *Leviathan*
John A. Hobson's *Imperialism: A Study*
Samuel P. Huntington's *The Clash of Civilizations and the Remaking of World Order*
Tony Judt's *Postwar: A History of Europe Since 1945*
David C. Kang's *China Rising: Peace, Power and Order in East Asia*
Paul Kennedy's *The Rise and Fall of Great Powers*
Robert Keohane's *After Hegemony*
Martin Luther King Jr.'s *Why We Can't Wait*
Henry Kissinger's *World Order: Reflections on the Character of Nations and the Course of History*
John Locke's *Two Treatises of Government*
Niccolò Machiavelli's *The Prince*
Thomas Robert Malthus's *An Essay on the Principle of Population*
Mahmood Mamdani's *Citizen and Subject: Contemporary Africa And The Legacy Of Late Colonialism*
Karl Marx's *Capital*
John Stuart Mill's *On Liberty*
John Stuart Mill's *Utilitarianism*
Hans Morgenthau's *Politics Among Nations*
Thomas Paine's *Common Sense*
Thomas Paine's *Rights of Man*
Thomas Piketty's *Capital in the Twenty-First Century*
Robert D. Putman's *Bowling Alone*
John Rawls's *Theory of Justice*
Jean-Jacques Rousseau's *The Social Contract*
Theda Skocpol's *States and Social Revolutions*
Adam Smith's *The Wealth of Nations*
Sun Tzu's *The Art of War*
Henry David Thoreau's *Civil Disobedience*
Thucydides's *The History of the Peloponnesian War*
Kenneth Waltz's *Theory of International Politics*
Max Weber's *Politics as a Vocation*
Odd Arne Westad's *The Global Cold War: Third World Interventions And The Making Of Our Times*

POSTCOLONIAL STUDIES

Roland Barthes's *Mythologies*
Frantz Fanon's *Black Skin, White Masks*
Homi K. Bhabha's *The Location of Culture*
Gustavo Gutiérrez's *A Theology of Liberation*
Edward Said's *Orientalism*
Gayatri Chakravorty Spivak's *Can the Subaltern Speak?*

PSYCHOLOGY

Gordon Allport's *The Nature of Prejudice*
Alan Baddeley & Graham Hitch's *Aggression: A Social Learning Analysis*
Albert Bandura's *Aggression: A Social Learning Analysis*
Leon Festinger's *A Theory of Cognitive Dissonance*
Sigmund Freud's *The Interpretation of Dreams*
Betty Friedan's *The Feminine Mystique*
Michael R. Gottfredson & Travis Hirschi's *A General Theory of Crime*
Eric Hoffer's *The True Believer: Thoughts on the Nature of Mass Movements*
William James's *Principles of Psychology*
Elizabeth Loftus's *Eyewitness Testimony*
A. H. Maslow's *A Theory of Human Motivation*
Stanley Milgram's *Obedience to Authority*
Steven Pinker's *The Better Angels of Our Nature*
Oliver Sacks's *The Man Who Mistook His Wife For a Hat*
Richard Thaler & Cass Sunstein's *Nudge: Improving Decisions About Health, Wealth and Happiness*
Amos Tversky's *Judgment under Uncertainty: Heuristics and Biases*
Philip Zimbardo's *The Lucifer Effect*

SCIENCE

Rachel Carson's *Silent Spring*
William Cronon's *Nature's Metropolis: Chicago And The Great West*
Alfred W. Crosby's *The Columbian Exchange*
Charles Darwin's *On the Origin of Species*
Richard Dawkin's *The Selfish Gene*
Thomas Kuhn's *The Structure of Scientific Revolutions*
Geoffrey Parker's *Global Crisis: War, Climate Change and Catastrophe in the Seventeenth Century*
Mathis Wackernagel & William Rees's *Our Ecological Footprint*

SOCIOLOGY

Michelle Alexander's *The New Jim Crow: Mass Incarceration in the Age of Colorblindness*
Gordon Allport's *The Nature of Prejudice*
Albert Bandura's *Aggression: A Social Learning Analysis*
Hanna Batatu's *The Old Social Classes And The Revolutionary Movements Of Iraq*
Ha-Joon Chang's *Kicking Away the Ladder*
W. E. B. Du Bois's *The Souls of Black Folk*
Émile Durkheim's *On Suicide*
Frantz Fanon's *Black Skin, White Masks*
Frantz Fanon's *The Wretched of the Earth*
Eric Foner's *Reconstruction: America's Unfinished Revolution, 1863-1877*
Eugene Genovese's *Roll, Jordan, Roll: The World the Slaves Made*
Jack Goldstone's *Revolution and Rebellion in the Early Modern World*
Antonio Gramsci's *The Prison Notebooks*
Richard Herrnstein & Charles A Murray's *The Bell Curve: Intelligence and Class Structure in American Life*
Eric Hoffer's *The True Believer: Thoughts on the Nature of Mass Movements*
Jane Jacobs's *The Death and Life of Great American Cities*
Robert Lucas's *Why Doesn't Capital Flow from Rich to Poor Countries?*
Jay Macleod's *Ain't No Makin' It: Aspirations and Attainment in a Low Income Neighborhood*
Elaine May's *Homeward Bound: American Families in the Cold War Era*
Douglas McGregor's *The Human Side of Enterprise*
C. Wright Mills's *The Sociological Imagination*

Thomas Piketty's *Capital in the Twenty-First Century*
Robert D. Putman's *Bowling Alone*
David Riesman's *The Lonely Crowd: A Study of the Changing American Character*
Edward Said's *Orientalism*
Joan Wallach Scott's *Gender and the Politics of History*
Theda Skocpol's *States and Social Revolutions*
Max Weber's *The Protestant Ethic and the Spirit of Capitalism*

THEOLOGY

Augustine's *Confessions*
Benedict's *Rule of St Benedict*
Gustavo Gutiérrez's *A Theology of Liberation*
Carole Hillenbrand's *The Crusades: Islamic Perspectives*
David Hume's *Dialogues Concerning Natural Religion*
Immanuel Kant's *Religion within the Boundaries of Mere Reason*
Ernst Kantorowicz's *The King's Two Bodies: A Study in Medieval Political Theology*
Søren Kierkegaard's *The Sickness Unto Death*
C. S. Lewis's *The Abolition of Man*
Saba Mahmood's *The Politics of Piety: The Islamic Revival and the Feminist Subject*
Baruch Spinoza's *Ethics*
Keith Thomas's *Religion and the Decline of Magic*

COMING SOON

Chris Argyris's *The Individual and the Organisation*
Seyla Benhabib's *The Rights of Others*
Walter Benjamin's *The Work Of Art in the Age of Mechanical Reproduction*
John Berger's *Ways of Seeing*
Pierre Bourdieu's *Outline of a Theory of Practice*
Mary Douglas's *Purity and Danger*
Roland Dworkin's *Taking Rights Seriously*
James G. March's *Exploration and Exploitation in Organisational Learning*
Ikujiro Nonaka's *A Dynamic Theory of Organizational Knowledge Creation*
Griselda Pollock's *Vision and Difference*
Amartya Sen's *Inequality Re-Examined*
Susan Sontag's *On Photography*
Yasser Tabbaa's *The Transformation of Islamic Art*
Ludwig von Mises's *Theory of Money and Credit*

Macat Pairs

Analyse historical and modern issues from opposite sides of an argument. Pairs include:

INTERNATIONAL RELATIONS IN THE 21ST CENTURY

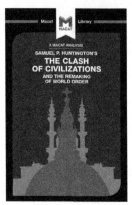

Samuel P. Huntington's
The Clash of Civilisations
In his highly influential 1996 book, Huntington offers a vision of a post-Cold War world in which conflict takes place not between competing ideologies but between cultures. The worst clash, he argues, will be between the Islamic world and the West: the West's arrogance and belief that its culture is a "gift" to the world will come into conflict with Islam's obstinacy and concern that its culture is under attack from a morally decadent "other."

Clash inspired much debate between different political schools of thought. But its greatest impact came in helping define American foreign policy in the wake of the 2001 terrorist attacks in New York and Washington.

Francis Fukuyama's
The End of History and the Last Man
Published in 1992, *The End of History and the Last Man* argues that capitalist democracy is the final destination for all societies. Fukuyama believed democracy triumphed during the Cold War because it lacks the "fundamental contradictions" inherent in communism and satisfies our yearning for freedom and equality. Democracy therefore marks the endpoint in the evolution of ideology, and so the "end of history." There will still be "events," but no fundamental change in ideology.

Macat Disciplines

Access the greatest ideas and thinkers across entire disciplines, including

MAN AND THE ENVIRONMENT

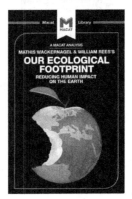

The Brundtland Report's, *Our Common Future*
Rachel Carson's, *Silent Spring*
James Lovelock's, *Gaia: A New Look at Life on Earth*
Mathis Wackernagel & William Rees's, *Our Ecological Footprint*

Macat analyses are available from all good bookshops and libraries.

Access hundreds of analyses through one, multimedia tool.
Join free for one month **library.macat.com**

Macat Pairs

*Analyse historical and modern issues
from opposite sides of an argument.
Pairs include:*

ARE WE FUNDAMENTALLY GOOD - OR BAD?

Steven Pinker's
The Better Angels of Our Nature

Stephen Pinker's gloriously optimistic 2011 book argues that, despite humanity's biological tendency toward violence, we are, in fact, less violent today than ever before. To prove his case, Pinker lays out pages of detailed statistical evidence. For him, much of the credit for the decline goes to the eighteenth-century Enlightenment movement, whose ideas of liberty, tolerance, and respect for the value of human life filtered down through society and affected how people thought. That psychological change led to behavioral change—and overall we became more peaceful. Critics countered that humanity could never overcome the biological urge toward violence; others argued that Pinker's statistics were flawed.

Philip Zimbardo's
The Lucifer Effect

Some psychologists believe those who commit cruelty are innately evil. Zimbardo disagrees. In *The Lucifer Effect*, he argues that sometimes good people do evil things simply because of the situations they find themselves in, citing many historical examples to illustrate his point. Zimbardo details his 1971 Stanford prison experiment, where ordinary volunteers playing guards in a mock prison rapidly became abusive. But he also describes the tortures committed by US army personnel in Iraq's Abu Ghraib prison in 2003—and how he himself testified in defence of one of those guards. committed by US army personnel in Iraq's Abu Ghraib prison in 2003—and how he himself testified in defence of one of those guards.

Macat analyses are available from all good bookshops and libraries.

Access hundreds of analyses through one, multimedia tool.
Join free for one month **library.macat.com**

Macat Pairs

*Analyse historical and modern issues
from opposite sides of an argument.
Pairs include:*

HOW WE RELATE TO EACH OTHER AND SOCIETY

Jean-Jacques Rousseau's
The Social Contract

Rousseau's famous work sets out the radical concept of the 'social contract': a give-and-take relationship between individual freedom and social order.

If people are free to do as they like, governed only by their own sense of justice, they are also vulnerable to chaos and violence. To avoid this, Rousseau proposes, they should agree to give up some freedom to benefit from the protection of social and political organization. But this deal is only just if societies are led by the collective needs and desires of the people, and able to control the private interests of individuals. For Rousseau, the only legitimate form of government is rule by the people.

Robert D. Putnam's
Bowling Alone

In *Bowling Alone*, Robert Putnam argues that Americans have become disconnected from one another and from the institutions of their common life, and investigates the consequences of this change.

Looking at a range of indicators, from membership in formal organizations to the number of invitations being extended to informal dinner parties, Putnam demonstrates that Americans are interacting less and creating less "social capital" – with potentially disastrous implications for their society.

It would be difficult to overstate the impact of *Bowling Alone*, one of the most frequently cited social science publications of the last half-century.

Macat analyses are available from all good bookshops and libraries.

Access hundreds of analyses through one, multimedia tool.
Join free for one month **library.macat.com**

Printed in the United States
by Baker & Taylor Publisher Services